MAKING

Career Decisions

THAT COUNT

A PRACTICAL GUIDE

SECOND EDITION

Darrell Anthony Luzzo

MT. HOOD COMMUNITY COLLEGE

Prentice
Hall

Upper Saddle River, New Jersey
Columbus, Ohio

Library of Congress Cataloging-in-Publication Data

Luzzo, Darrell Anthony.
    Making career decisions that count : a practical guide / Darrell Anthony Luzzo.—2nd ed.
      p. cm.
    Includes bibliographical references and index.
    ISBN 0-13-019143-4
    1. Vocational guidance.   II. Title.
HF5381 .L783 2002
650.14—dc21

2001021573

Vice President and Publisher: Jeffery W. Johnston
Acquisitions Editor: Sande Johnson
Assistant Editor: Cecilia Johnson
Production Editor: Holcomb Hathaway
Design Coordinator: Diane C. Lorenzo
Cover Designer: Andrew Lundberg
Cover Art: Artville
Production Manager: Pamela D. Bennett
Director of Marketing: Kevin Flanagan
Marketing Manager: Christina Quadhamer
Marketing Coordinator: Barbara Koontz

This book was set in Janson by Aerocraft Charter Art Service. It was printed
and bound by Banta Book Group. The cover was printed by Banta Book Group.

Prentice-Hall International (UK) Limited, *London*
Prentice-Hall of Australia Pty. Limited, *Sydney*
Prentice-Hall Canada Inc., *Toronto*
Prentice-Hall Hispanoamericana, S.A., *Mexico*
Prentice-Hall of India Private Limited, *New Delhi*
Prentice-Hall of Japan, Inc., *Tokyo*
Pearson Education Singapore Pte. Ltd.
Editora Prentice-Hall do Brasil, Ltda., *Rio de Janeiro*

10 9 8 7 6 5 4 3 2 1
ISBN 0-13-019143-4

Contents

4 what matters most?

5 making the pieces fit

6 traveling through the maze

7 facing the challenges head-on

8 decisions, decisions, decisions

9 lights, camera, action!

10 what next?

A appendix

B appendix

C appendix

D appendix

E appendix

Preface

Career decision making is a lifelong process. The experiences we have during childhood and adolescence help us develop attitudes about the world of work and form the basis of some of our earliest career aspirations. As we enter adulthood, our experiences, personality, skills, and values become increasingly relevant as we narrow our interests down to the two or three careers we're most likely to pursue. That's when a clear understanding of the career decision-making process becomes so important. As just about every career counselor will attest, the most fulfilling and rewarding career decisions are made by those who understand what the career decision-making process is all about.

The second edition of *Making Career Decisions That Count: A Practical Guide* is written specifically to help you learn more about the multifaceted nature of career decision making as you engage in various career exploration and planning activities. Case studies of career decision makers of all ages are integrated throughout the book to illustrate important concepts and clarify the complexity of the career decision-making process. Interesting and informative chapter exercises provide you with several hands-on opportunities to put your newfound knowledge into practice. You'll learn hundreds of useful strategies to help you make career decisions that will lead to satisfaction, stability, and success.

Chapter 1, "Understanding the World of Work," introduces students to Dr. Anne Roe's system for classifying careers and encourages students to keep up with labor trends and job projections as they learn more about various career decision-making strategies. Chapter 2, "The Developmental Process of Making Career Decisions," discusses Donald Super's theory of career development and includes detailed examples of the various stages of the career decision-making process. You'll learn firsthand that making satisfying career decisions requires an increased awareness of your career self-concept.

In Chapter 3, "Assessing Your Personality, Interests, Abilities, and Experiences," and Chapter 4, "Recognizing the Importance of Your Values," you'll complete several exercises designed to help you learn more about your personality, interests, experiences, skills, and values. Then, in Chapter 5, "Integrating Information About Yourself," you'll evaluate your career-related self-concept and make some initial career decisions based on the results of assessments you'll complete in Chapters 3 and 4. As Chapter 5 concludes, you'll be encouraged to narrow your list of career options to the four or five that seem most worthy of continued exploration.

Chapter 6, "Methods of Career Exploration," presents information about multiple resources that can be used for gathering career-related information. The chapter includes descriptions of the *Occupational Outlook Handbook*, the recently developed O*NET system, Internet resources, and more than 20 other sources of information that you'll find useful. The chapter also discusses helpful hints and strategies regarding informational interviewing, job shadowing, and the importance of part-time and volunteer work experiences as valuable methods of career exploration.

Chapter 7, "Identifying and Overcoming the Hurdles," invites you to think constructively about the role of barriers in the career decision-making process. After learning about the differences between real and perceived, internal and external barriers, you'll complete a series of exercises to assist you in identifying career-related barriers and developing effective strategies for overcoming them.

With an increased awareness of your self-concept and a clearer understanding of the career decision-making process, you'll be prepared to narrow your career options down even further in Chapter 8, "Making a Tentative Career Decision." After emphasizing that career decisions are usually still tentative at this point in the process, the chapter introduces a useful, systematic method of analyzing career options. The career analysis exercise in this chapter will enable you to select the one career choice that seems most appropriate at this point. Chapter 8 also includes an expanded discussion of selecting a major to help you better understand the link between career goals and college majors. Then, in Chapter 9, "Creating a Career Activities Timeline," you'll learn about the importance of setting short- and long-term goals related to your career choices and develop specific strategies for accomplishing those goals.

Chapter 10, "Looking and Planning Ahead," presents an overview of the stages of career development that follow career exploration. You'll be encouraged to refine the career decision-making process as necessary to meet your own individual needs.

In addition to providing you with the latest information about the world of work; updated assessments of career interests, skills, and experiences; and expanded coverage of career information resources, this second edition also includes two new features that appear at the end of each chapter. These two features are "Surfing the Web with a Purpose" and "Questions for Critical Thought." "Surfing the Web with a Purpose" provides a listing of several Internet sites that are useful in career exploration and planning and are relevant to the concepts covered in the chapter. A brief description of what you'll find at each Web site accompanies each listing.

The "Questions for Critical Thought" feature at the end of each chapter gives you an opportunity to critically evaluate the information presented throughout the book. As college and university professors and researchers have discovered over the years, the more critically you're able to think about and process new information, the more apt you are to remember and apply that information over time.

For readers who are interested in obtaining part-time, volunteer, or full-time work experience as a means of career exploration, Appendix D summarizes several job search strategies to help you identify and seek employment opportunities. And, finally, Appendix E includes a questionnaire to assist you in evaluating the degree to which your current (or future) employment gives you the satisfaction and enjoyment that you would ideally experience in a job.

Instructors using this text in class will want to make sure they receive a copy of the *Instructor's Manual and Resource Guide* that accompanies *Making Career Decisions That Count: A Practical Guide*. Both seasoned veterans who have taught career-planning and exploration courses for many years and rookies who are teaching the course for the very first time will appreciate the comprehensive nature of the *Instructor's Manual and Resource Guide*. Included in each chapter of the *Instructor's Manual and Resource Guide* (corresponding with each individual chapter of the book) are chapter overviews, learning objectives, key concepts, proposed lecture outlines, suggested activities, and resource materials. The manual also provides instructors with sample course syllabi, transparency masters, a final exam, contact information for publishers of career resource materials, and an expanded listing of useful Internet sources and World Wide Web sites related to career planning and exploration.

Helping college students make career decisions that will provide them with satisfaction and success was first and foremost in my mind as I prepared both the first and second editions of this book. To that end, it is my sincere hope that those who read the book and invest an appropriate amount of time and energy into the process will be well on the road to making career decisions that count!

ACKNOWLEDGMENTS

I am indebted to numerous individuals whose assistance during the preparation of this book was invaluable. First and foremost, I am extremely grateful to each and every member of the staff at Prentice Hall. Their dedication to the success of this project was apparent at every stage of the process. The guidance and support provided by Sande Johnson is especially noteworthy. I also appreciate the helpful comments and suggestions of the three reviewers of the manuscript: Garry Klein (ACT, Inc.), Linda Schlotthauer (Mt. San Jacinto Community College, California), and Dr. Linda Scharf (Miami Dade Community College). I also wish to thank the many students, professors, career counselors, and clients who have suggested ways to improve the contents of the first edition of the book. I am confident that you'll benefit from the incorporation of their ideas into this edition. I would like to extend special gratitude for the guidance, direction, and inspiration provided over the years by two of my colleagues, Drs. Charles Healy and Mark Savickas, for whom I hold the highest respect and professional admiration. Most of all, I wish to express my thanks and appreciation to my gorgeous wife and eternal companion, Tanya, and to our nine beautiful children: Nicholas, Stacia, Logan, Braden, Kira, Tara, Emalise, Tannan, and Emma. They remind me each and every day what life is really all about!

It's a jungle out there

UNDERSTANDING THE WORLD OF WORK

As you begin the process of making career decisions, it's important to have a good understanding of the world of work with all of its components and uncertainties. The purpose of this chapter is to introduce you to the always changing, ever dynamic world of work. We'll begin the process by discussing a system of categorizing different work environments and career domains. Then we will discuss the importance of recognizing certain trends in the world of work and of gathering and organizing occupational information as you consider various career opportunities. You'll also have the opportunity in this chapter to reflect on some of your long-term goals as you begin to think about the things you'd like to accomplish over the next several years.

AN OVERVIEW OF THE WORLD OF WORK

In previous generations many Americans selected a single occupation in their late teens or early twenties and often remained in that career all the way through retirement. Decisions about where to work were based mostly on geographical location and family history rather than personal values or potential career advancement.

Today, there's plenty of evidence that times are constantly changing. Most people now struggle during their late teens and early twenties, as well as during other periods in their lives, as they search for the career that promises the most fulfillment and satisfaction. If you're anything like the typical American worker, you'll change careers between five and seven times during your working years. Career changes that involve working for a new company, relocating, and sometimes even changing a career direction altogether are becoming a reality for more and more people each year. Many of today's high school and college graduates, as well as others who are considering making career changes, are on a quest to find careers that will provide personal satisfaction and the potential for professional growth and development.

The typical American changes careers five to seven times.

The world of work that you're a part of (or will soon be entering) contains thousands of different occupations. Some occupations require little or no formal training beyond high school. Others require several years of educational training and multiple years of experience. Some occupations involve working with your hands or working outdoors. Others involve working with people or solving complex, scientific problems. Some jobs provide structure and routine in the workplace. Others provide the opportunity for artistic and creative expression. Figuring out which career is going to provide you with the greatest degree of satisfaction and enjoyment may not be such a simple feat!

As you engage in the process of making career decisions, one of the first things you'll need to do is increase your understanding of the world of work. Suppose for a moment that you entered a contest and won a free vacation to Mazatlan, Mexico. After getting over the initial shock of winning, you'd probably want to know several things about Mazatlan as you prepared for your trip. The average temperature and climate, types of leisure activities, and modes of transportation would all be important to know in order to have a fun and enjoyable vacation. Making career decisions, although perhaps not quite as exciting as a trip to Mexico, also requires important planning and investigation. Just as you'd want to learn about the environment of Mazatlan to prepare for your vacation, you'll want to learn as much as you can about the world of work as you prepare to make career decisions that count.

CLASSIFYING WORK ENVIRONMENTS

There are many different ways to organize the world of work. One of the most well-known systems for classifying work environments was developed by Dr. John L. Holland, whose system includes six primary work environments: *Realistic* jobs that involve working with your hands or in outdoor settings, *Investigative* jobs that entail searching for solutions to complex problems, *Artistic* environments that encourage creativity and personal expression, *Social* settings that provide you with the opportunity to teach and help other people, *Enterprising* jobs in which you manage or persuade others, and *Conventional* work environments characterized by organization and planning. Dr. Holland's classification system is used by many career counselors throughout the world to help people make career decisions. You may come across Dr. Holland's method of categorizing careers as you're exposed to various career assessments and other sources of occupational information.

Another well-known system for classifying work environments was developed by Dr. Anne Roe in the 1950s when she discovered that existing classification systems were inadequate. She was troubled that none of the classifications of occupations at that time seemed to follow a logical framework of organization. Based on years of research and experience, Dr. Roe developed a classification system that includes eight occupational groups and work environments.

Service. This work environment involves serving and attending to the personal tastes, needs, and welfare of others. The focus is on doing something to help other people. Examples of occupations that fall into this work environment include social work, counseling, and many domestic and protective services, such as law enforcement and fire protection services.

Business Contact. The occupations included in this work environment involve the face-to-face sale of material goods or services. As in the Service category, person-to-person relationships are important, but in the Business Contact area these relationships are focused on persuading other people to engage in a particular course of action—such as buying a product—rather than on helping others. Examples of careers that fall into this work category include sales, public relations, marketing, advertising, and real estate.

Organization. This work environment is concerned primarily with the organization and efficient functioning of commercial enterprises and government activities, where the quality of person-to-person relationships is more formalized. Managerial and administrative careers in business, industry, and government are included in this work environment. Examples of people in this area include small-business owners, accountants, hotel managers, and bankers.

Technology. The Technology work environment focuses on the production, maintenance, and transportation of commodities and utilities. Interpersonal relationships are of relatively little value. Instead, the focus is on dealing with *things* as opposed to dealing with *people*. Careers in engineering, machine trades, and the transportation industry belong in this environment. Examples include mechanic, carpenter, aerospace engineer, electrician, and construction worker.

Outdoors. This occupational group includes careers primarily concerned with the cultivation, preservation, and gathering of natural resources and animal welfare. As in the Technology work environment, many Outdoors careers provide few opportunities for emphasizing interpersonal relationships. Examples of Outdoors careers include landscape architects, forest rangers, horticulturists, tree surgeons, and gardeners.

Science. Science-related careers include occupations primarily concerned with scientific theory and its application to real-world problems. Medical doctors, physicists, research psychologists, university professors, and chiropractors are among the many professionals who are directly associated with this work environment.

General Culture. The General Culture category involves careers that are primarily concerned with the preservation and transmission of the general culture and heritage. The emphasis in this type of work environment is on human activities collectively rather than on individual person-to-person relationships. This group includes occupations in education, journalism, law, and careers that fall into a category often referred to as "the humanities." Examples of careers that fall into the General Culture category include school teacher, reporter, historian, lawyer, and newscaster.

Arts and Entertainment. Occupations included in this work environment involve the use of special skills in the creative arts and the world of entertainment. In this category, the focus is on a relationship between one person (or an organized group) and the general public. A wide range of careers falls into the Arts and Entertainment work environment, including examples such as designers and interior decorators, professional athletes, actors, musicians, and screenwriters.

To help you get a better sense of Dr. Roe's classification system, Table 1.1 summarizes the eight different work environments.

As you progress through the stages of the career decision-making process, you'll learn more about determining which particular work environments are likely to provide you with the most personal satisfaction and success. But first we have a few other important issues to discuss.

TABLE 1.1	*Summary of work environments.*

WORK ENVIRONMENT	SAMPLE OCCUPATIONS	CHARACTERISTICS OF PEOPLE WHO LIKE WORKING IN THESE ENVIRONMENTS
Service	Social worker, Police officer, Family counselor, Occupational therapist	Enjoy serving and attending to the personal tastes, needs, and welfare of other people; obtain a strong sense of satisfaction from helping and/or protecting other people.
Business Contact	Real estate agent, Salesperson, Insurance agent, Public relations specialist	Enjoy persuading other people to engage in a particular course of action, such as the purchase of a commodity or service.
Organization	Employment manager, Human resources director, Business executive, Small-business owner	Enjoy engaging in tasks that involve a high level of organization and precision; often satisfied by supervising or managing others.
Technology	Repair Person, Mechanic, Civil engineer, Carpenter	Enjoy producing, transporting, and/or fixing things; more satisfied working with tools and objects than with people.
Outdoors	Forest ranger, Horticulturalist, Wildlife specialist, Farmer	Enjoy working in outdoor settings; often favor working with animals and plants rather than with people.
Science	Chiropractor, X-ray technician, Dentist, Pediatrician	Enjoy working with scientific theory and its application to real-world problems.
General Culture	Lawyer, High school teacher, Librarian, Historian	Enjoy interacting with groups of people in an effort to preserve and/or transmit knowledge and cultural heritage.
Arts and Entertainment	Interior decorator, Artist Professional athlete, Actor	Enjoy environments that provide opportunities for artistic expression and/or the use of special skills in an entertainment industry.

WORLD OF WORK: FORECASTS AND TRENDS

In addition to learning about ways to classify work environments, making effective career decisions also requires you to increase your awareness of trends and forecasts about the future regarding the world of work. In recent years, many people have engaged in the process of predicting the economic and demographic employment trends of the 21st century. Some of their predictions have been no more accurate than a daily horoscope reading. Others, however, have provided important information that can be very useful as you consider various career opportunities.

One of the best things you can do at this point is get in the habit of going to the library or accessing the Internet every now and then to read about the world of work and gain a better idea of career projections. Just as you might window shop to check out the latest fashions, skimming through up-to-date occupational information and economic projections will give you a clearer picture of the world of work.

It will be important for you to gather various types of information during *all* stages of your career decision-making process. Fortunately, numerous sources are available to you for increasing your understanding of work trends. Among these resources are best-selling books and popular magazines that often contain useful articles and feature stories related to the world of work.

Perhaps most relevant to your specific career decisions are sources of information that offer projections about the types of industries that will see the greatest growth in the future. Based on recent trends, the U. S. Department of Labor believes that the fastest-growing occupations over the next several years will include positions in the allied health and service fields (e.g., home health aides, physical therapists, human service workers) and information analysis (e.g., computer systems analysts, operations research analysts).

Of course, these are only projections. Obtaining accurate, up-to-date information about employment opportunities will be important as you continue to make career decisions. In fact, keeping a close watch on employment trends and changes in the world of work may be the key to your own personal career satisfaction and success.

You'll want to gather information about the world of work during all stages of the career decision-making process.

In addition to books and periodic reports published by the U. S. Department of Labor, various other publications provide a good overview of the world of work. One way to find out about current information is to read magazines, such as *Money* or *Fortune*, that are primarily devoted to covering labor issues. These types of magazines often include feature articles devoted to employment issues and job projections. Even weekly news magazines such as *Time*, *Newsweek*, and *U.S. News & World Report* can supply you with important information about the world of work.

As you begin to gather information, you might also be surprised at how helpful some newspapers can be. Larger newspapers, such as the *Wall Street Journal*, *USA Today*, and the *New York Times*, usually include stories related to the world of work. Your own local newspaper might be informative as well. Reading through the business section of my local newspaper the other day, I found an excellent article on local labor trends. The story presented up-to-date information about employment opportunities in various industries located in my community.

Another quick and easy way to find out what categories of careers are on the rise is to see what types of training programs are being offered at your local community college or adult education center. The kinds of courses and programs that are popular at a local community college or adult education center often reflect the kinds of skills that employers in that region are looking for.

Yet another source that will become increasingly valuable to you as you narrow your list of career options is the *Occupational Outlook Handbook* (OOH), published by the U. S. Department of Labor. The handbook is printed every couple of years and is available at nearly every public and college library. It provides a variety of detailed information about hundreds of occupations. You'll find especially helpful details about working conditions, salary ranges, educational and training requirements, and employment projections for the next several years. Figure 1.1 shows an example of the kind of information you'll find in the OOH.

Yet another very useful resource is the Department of Labor's recently developed Web site for occupational information, O*NET. O*NET features a variety of informational guides to assist you throughout the career exploration and planning process. The O*NET Web site is upgraded and expanded on a regular basis, offering visitors up-to-date information about the world of work that can be quite valuable during career decision making. The O*NET Web site can be found at www.doleta.gov.programs/onet.

GATHERING AND EVALUATING EMPLOYMENT INFORMATION AND SUPPORT

As you gather employment information from these and other resources, the kinds of questions you'll want to answer include the following:

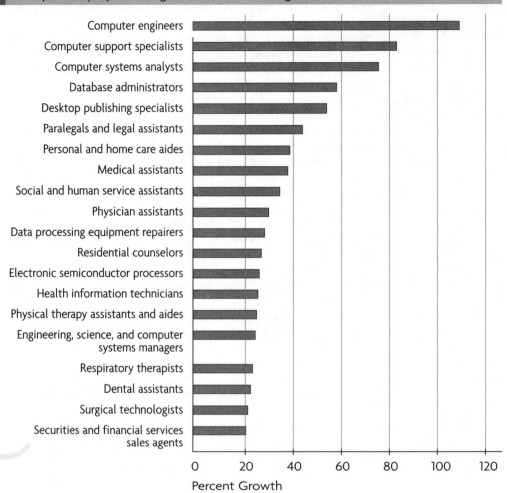

FIGURE 1.1   *Occupations projected to grow the fastest through 2008.*

Source: *Occupational Outlook Handbook.*

- How many jobs will be available in the career areas that I'm considering?
- Will there be ample employment opportunities in the geographical region where I want to live?
- What about salary expectations? Will I make enough money to support my lifestyle needs and wants?
- Is growth projected within a specific career area I'm interested in, or is a decline more likely?

Along with reading relevant books and magazines and periodically reviewing information from the Department of Labor, you'll benefit from keeping up to date with current local and global affairs and talking with friends and colleagues about career-related questions.

You should also contact associations and organizations in your area that might be able to offer you support on the basis of your particular background and interests. Many college and university campuses, for example, have organized groups that might be particularly relevant to you. Perhaps joining a student club made up of individuals who share your ethnic background or religious preference would be helpful. Women's centers, international student centers, and offices for students with disabilities are other resources that you may want to consider consulting for support and direction regarding your career choice.

Depending on your level of familiarity and comfort with computers, you might also consider using the Internet as a rich source of occupational information. Many Web sites offer endless information about employment projections and trends, facts about various careers, and current job openings in various fields. If you have the opportunity to "surf the Net," you'll be sure to find lots of helpful occupational information that will serve you well throughout the career exploration process. At the end of each chapter you'll find an annotated list of useful Web sites you may want to consider visiting to supplement the information presented in this book. These lists give you a sort of "head start" in locating Internet resources to support and enhance your career exploration and planning experience.

Be as organized as possible as you engage in the career decision-making process

The information you'll be gathering from the various sources discussed thus far will become increasingly important as you continue the career decision-making process. You might want to consider organizing the information so that it will be helpful to you in the future. Use a filing cabinet or a sturdy box to collect newspaper and magazine articles. Be sure to keep this information where you normally keep your other class materials. Use filing folders or notebooks to separate information into categories. General work trends can be stored in one folder or notebook, employment opportunities in another notebook, salary expectations in another, and so forth.

Throughout this book, you'll be encouraged to be as organized as possible as you engage in the career decision-making process. Researchers have consistently found that the most effective career decisions are carried out by those who invest an appropriate amount of time and energy in them. Career decisions can be extremely rewarding and personally fulfilling if you're willing to be an active participant in the process.

Terry and Kelsey   CONSIDER

Consider the cases of Terry and Kelsey, two college graduates preparing to enter the world of work. Both majored in business at a reputable institution in the Midwest. A few months before graduation, Terry and Kelsey both decided that they wanted to find a job on the West Coast. After identifying this goal, Terry began actively engaging in the career decision-making process. To learn about the different types of business-related jobs that were available in various regions of the country, Terry met with several professors at the college and with a few prominent business leaders in the community. They provided Terry with information about the kinds of jobs currently available in the business world and offered helpful advice about job interviewing and resume writing. Terry also contacted several potential employers on the West Coast, forwarding copies of an updated resume and making follow-up phone calls to inquire about possible openings.

Kelsey, on the other hand, never actively engaged in learning about employment prospects or workforce trends. Kelsey figured that the college placement office would provide that information. There were no meetings with college faculty members, no contacts with local businesspersons, and no interaction with personnel offices of West Coast companies.

Needless to say, Terry was much more successful in securing a position than Kelsey. Two weeks after graduation, Terry moved to San Francisco and began working for a Fortune 500 firm. Kelsey, however, was unable to obtain employment on the West Coast and eventually found a job closer to home.

THE IMPORTANCE OF GOAL SETTING IN CAREER PLANNING

The importance of career planning cannot be emphasized enough. In Chapter 2, you'll learn more about the process of career development and the reasons why career planning is critical. In the meantime, I want to assure you that the effort you're willing to devote to making career decisions at this point in your life will benefit you for many years to come.

Think for a moment about the role that work and careers play in our lives. On any given day, most people work at least eight or nine hours. Most people also sleep about seven or eight hours a day, which leaves about eight hours for other activities. When you factor in driving time to and from work and time to prepare mentally for work at the start of the day and to wind down once you return home, you quickly begin to realize that a fairly large chunk of your waking hours is spent engaged in work-related activities. In fact, it has been suggested that most of us spend the *majority* of our waking hours during our adult lives engaged in work-related activities. That's probably why selecting a career is considered such an important task. It's important to realize that the time and energy you devote to this process now will result in direct dividends to you for many years to come.

Most of us spend the majority of our adult lives engaged in work-related activities.

To set the stage, take a few minutes to complete Exercise 1.1, "Short-Term and Long-Range Goal Setting."

As with all of the exercises in this book, it's important that you be honest with yourself. Don't let the expectations of others interfere with your own, personal understanding of who you are and what it is that *you* want. As we'll be discussing later in the book, family influences and the expectations of others can sometimes serve as barriers to effective career decision making. You'll get the most out of these exercises if you're able to reflect on your own personal thoughts and feelings and answer the questions as honestly as you possibly can.

You'll want to complete these exercises when you've got plenty of time and don't feel too tired. Try to find a quiet, peaceful spot for reflection. Try playing soothing music while you complete the exercises or choosing a special physical space that you find particularly comfortable. Sometimes visually imagining a peaceful atmosphere can help. The key is to create an environment free of distractions and interruptions. That way you'll be able to think about important issues as you prepare to make the best career decisions that you possibly can.

EXERCISE 1.1	*SHORT-TERM AND LONG-RANGE GOAL SETTING*

Consider the next 10 to 20 years of your life. There are probably many things that you'd like to accomplish during that period of time. Some of your goals may be best characterized as short-term goals and involve things you'd like to do this month or later this year. Others are probably long-term and include things you'd like to accomplish over the next several years. Many of your goals will be related to your hobbies and interests; others might involve your family and friends. Some are career-related, whereas others are probably best characterized as leisure activities.

Don't focus exclusively at this point on career goals. Instead, think of the *many* different kinds of things that you'd like to do in *all* areas of your life. Be sure to consider personal goals that involve only you and your personal growth and development as well as those goals that involve others in your life.

A. Take some time to reflect on your future. List below the many goals (both short-term and long-range) that you'd like to accomplish within the next 20 years or so. Try to state your goals in the language that you usually use. Try not to list your goals in general terms (such as, "I want to be successful"). Instead, state your goals in specific ways (such as, "I want to complete my bachelor's degree within the next five years"). Go ahead and dream, too. Even if some of your goals may be idealistic, this is a time to brainstorm about anything and everything that you'd like to accomplish. (We'll worry about realistic expectations later.)

_____

_____

_____

_____

_____

_____

_____

_____

_____

_____

_____

_____

_____

_____

_____

B. Now go back through your list of long-range goals. Place each goal that you've listed into one of the specific time frames listed below.

Goals You Hope to Accomplish Within the Next 10 to 20 Years

_____

_____

_____

_____

_____

Goals You Hope to Accomplish Within the Next 5 to 10 Years

_____

_____

_____

_____

_____

Goals You Hope to Accomplish Within the Next 3 to 5 Years

_____

_____

_____

_____

_____

Goals You Hope to Accomplish Within the Next 2 to 3 Years

_____

_____

_____

_____

_____

Goals You Hope to Accomplish Within the Next Year

_____

_____

_____

_____

_____

C. Over the next several days, try to think of other goals that you might like to accomplish. Add these goals to your list to make it as complete as possible. Allow yourself the flexibility of changing some of your goals, too. These are meant to be guidelines and will serve as the basis for further self-exploration that you'll participate in throughout the career decision-making process.

D. You'll be referring back to your list of goals later in the book. In the meantime, try to remember that your career is just one of the many aspects of your life that deserves attention. Don't forget to devote ample time and energy working toward other personal goals as you continue your quest to make career decisions that count.

SURFING THE WEB WITH A PURPOSE

The Web sites listed below can provide further information about the material in this chapter. The Internet changes all the time, so it's quite possible that a few of the addresses here may no longer be valid by the time you read this book. For the most part, however, you're likely to benefit greatly by investing a few minutes to give these sites a try!

http://stats.bls.gov/emphome.htm This site, sponsored by the U. S. Bureau of Labor Statistics, provides a host of links regarding employment projections—all based on data collected by the Bureau. Categories of information you will find at this site include News Releases, Data, and Publications and Other Documentation.

www.dol.gov/dol/asp/public/futurework/welcome.html Sponsored by the U. S. Department of Labor, this site focuses on trends and challenges for work in the 21st century. Entitled "Futurework," the site includes text reports of the Secretary of Labor's recent addresses as well as the full text of "Futurework," a recent report about work trends published by the Department of Labor.

http://lmi-imt.hrdc-drhc.gc.ca This site, sponsored by the Human Resources Department of Canada, provides labor market information for Canada.

www.rileyguide.com The Riley Guide is one of the oldest and most extensive Internet career tools available on the Web. It includes information about where to find jobs, salary surveys, an A-to-Z index of job positions, help for researching careers and employers, and a guide to Internet job hunting. Because of its comprehensiveness, you might want to get to know the site now for future reference and use.

QUESTIONS FOR CRITICAL THOUGHT

1. Why is planning such an important part of the career exploration and planning process?
2. How can an awareness of job projections and economic factors help you make more effective career decisions?
3. How can you begin to figure out which career or work environment is most likely to provide you with lasting satisfaction, stability, and success?
4. What resources exist in your local community that can be useful to you as you gather information about the world of work?

Step by step

2

Just about everyone would agree that before traveling to a distant location it's always a good idea to be sure you know how to get there. The same is true regarding the process of career decision making. If you share the hope that most people do (namely that your career choice will bring you satisfaction, stability, and success), then it's important to learn how to reach your career destination.

The purpose of this chapter is to introduce you to the developmental process of making career decisions. In particular, you'll learn about the process of career and life development as conceptualized by the world-renowned Dr. Donald Super. You'll learn about the various stages of career development that we experience throughout our lives and the tasks associated with each stage. You'll also have the chance to reflect on your past work experiences and consider their role in shaping your career interests and values. Finally, you'll be given the opportunity to determine which stage of career development you're currently experiencing and which career exploration activities presented in this book are most relevant to your life situation.

THE PROCESS OF CAREER DEVELOPMENT

When I was in seventh grade, I completed a two-day workshop in my social studies class that was designed to introduce junior high school students to various career options. I remember thinking to myself that the career choice I selected as a result of that workshop (priest) was going to be the career I would "have to" pursue later in life. Now, over 20 years later, I'm a college dean, a nationally certified counselor, and a father of nine children—a far cry from the career choice and life in general I envisioned back in seventh grade!

Career decision making is a lifelong process.

Making career decisions is anything but a static process. Decisions that you make throughout your life, experiences that you have with other people, and the types of environments in which you live all contribute to your career development. Career decision making is a lifelong process that *everyone* experiences over and over again.

If you had met with a career counselor in the early 1900s, that counselor probably would have given you a few assessments, analyzed the results, and told you which occupations (based on your interests, skills, and values) were worth your time to consider. Odds are that you would have followed the counselor's advice and entered a career that you probably would have remained in for the next 40 years of your life. In more recent years career counselors have learned that times have most certainly changed. It has become extremely rare for a person to make a career decision around age 18 and stick with it for life. With rapidly shifting changes in the economy and the constant creation of new jobs and technologies, millions of people find themselves reliving the career decision-making process year after year. That's why many career counselors use the term "career development" when referring to the process of making career decisions. It's a lifelong, developmental process with different activities and tasks associated with each stage along the way. That's why it's so important that you learn about the *process* involved in making effective career decisions.

DONALD SUPER'S THEORY OF CAREER DEVELOPMENT

As with just about any other area of human behavior, counselors and psychologists have developed several different theories in an attempt to explain what happens during the career decision-making process. One of the most universally accepted theories of career decision making was developed by Dr. Donald Super, whose theory of career and life development was one of the first to describe career decision making as a developmental process that spans one's entire lifetime. Dr. Super believed that the degree to which a given individual's career development is successful depends—at least in part—on how well that person is able to identify and implement her or his career self-concept.

Your career self-concept is a product of the interaction of your personality, interests, experiences, skills, and values, and the ways in which you integrate these characteristics into your various life roles.

According to Dr. Super, your career self-concept is directly influenced by your personality, abilities, interests, experiences, and values. Suppose, for example, that you have the natural ability to listen attentively to others while they're speaking. Suppose that you're also good at expressing concern for others and helping them find solutions to their problems. These particular attributes suggest that a career in one of the helping professions might be appropriate. However, if you have little or no interest in the helping professions, then spending hours and hours exploring such career options would probably be a waste of time. Dr. Super argued that the best career choices people can make are those that provide avenues for implementing as many parts of their self-concept as possible.

Your career self-concept, according to Dr. Super, is a product of the interaction of your personality, interests, experiences, skills, and values, and the ways in which you integrate these characteristics into your various life roles. As you experience new situations in life, meet new people, and learn more about the world of work, you're likely to develop a new set of interests, unlock new possibilities of expressing your self-concept, and find new ways of integrating your values into the career choice process.

If you're like most people, it's very likely that at many times throughout your life you'll find yourself in situations that require you to reconsider your career direction. This may be the result of economic changes or trends. Perhaps it will be related to new technological advances. It may simply be "time for a change." Your interests may change. Your values may change. Even aspects of your personality may change. That's why it's so important for you to learn how to make good career decisions. That way, no matter when the need or desire for a career change arises, you'll be ready to tackle the challenge.

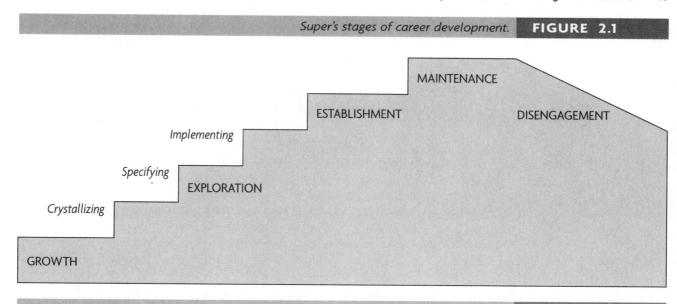

Dr. Super described career development as consisting of five distinct stages, which are depicted in Figure 2.1 and summarized in the adjacent box. Whether you're engaging in the career decision-making process for the first time or recycling through the process for the tenth time, you'll probably be able to determine which stage best characterizes your current situation.

Growth

According to Dr. Super, the first stage of career development is the **growth** stage. During this stage people form attitudes and behaviors that are important for the development of their self-concept and learn about the general nature of the world of work. According to Dr. Super, our interactions with the social environment influence our personal expectations and goals. Experiences we have with other people and the work we are exposed to throughout our lives have a direct impact on the development of our career-related attitudes and our beliefs about the world of work. Dr. Super believed that all children and young adolescents are in the growth stage of career development. But younger people aren't the only ones forming attitudes about careers and learning about the world of work. Many adults—especially those who are still learning about career opportunities—find themselves in the growth stage, too.

Summary of Dr. Super's Stages of Career Development

Stage	Basic Focus Associated with Each Stage
Growth	Learning about the world of work as you increase your awareness of your personality, interests, abilities, experiences, and values.
Exploration	Crystallizing, specifying, and implementing a career choice.
Establishment	Gaining work experiences and evaluating your experiences in occupations associated with your career choice.
Maintenance	Developing stability within a chosen career field as you seek ways to improve working conditions and increase skills.
Disengagement	Exploring new ways to spend your time away from your current work environment; might include a career change or retirement from full-time employment.

Lauren **CONSIDER**

Lauren, a student I worked with several years ago, was a 21-year-old woman characteristic of someone in the growth stage of career development. She was in her junior year at a university where she had been majoring in education. Lauren was the first person in her family ever to go to college. Her mother and father were extremely supportive of her desire to obtain a college degree, but—primarily because of their lack of college experience—they weren't able to offer Lauren sound advice and direction regarding the educational process.

Nevertheless, Lauren was aware that career counseling and academic advising services were available at the university, so she decided to meet with me to begin that process. One of the first things we talked about was Lauren's decision to major in education. She explained to me that she originally decided education would be a good avenue to pursue because there seemed to be a lot of available teaching jobs in the area. It became very clear rather quickly, however, that Lauren was not really interested in a career in education. She wanted to find a major that would be more appropriate for her.

As we continued working together, it became apparent that Lauren was still in the process of forming some general attitudes about work and was learning about her self-concept. Although she had not yet begun the actual career exploration process, she was ready and willing to engage in various exploratory activities. Her willingness to take the time and expend the necessary effort to make an effective career decision proved helpful. Today Lauren is successfully employed as a speech pathologist and finds great satisfaction in her work.

Exploration

The second stage of the career development process is **exploration,** considered by many to be the heart of the career decision-making process. Dr. Super described the exploration stage of career development as consisting of three major developmental tasks: crystallizing, specifying, and implementing a career choice.

Crystallizing

During the crystallizing task, career "dreaming" occurs. Some of the options identified during the crystallizing period might someday be realized, but most of the options identified at this point are more "idealistic" than "realistic."

CONSIDER *Jesse*

A student I worked with several years ago was engaging in the **crystallizing** task of career exploration when we met. Jesse had just graduated from high school, where he had been active in several different clubs and activities. He had served as the president of his school's Black Students Association, had been successful in speech and debate, and had lettered in several different sports. His mother had convinced him that before going to college he should meet with a career counselor.

As Jesse and I discussed some of the careers he was interested in pursuing, Jesse shared with me his strong desire to achieve numerous career goals before turning 35. He was confident that he would encounter few problems as he tried to become a U. S. Senator, the CEO of a Fortune 500 company, and an all-pro running back . . . all by the time he turned 35! Somehow he had developed the idea that he could accomplish every single one of these goals in less than 15 years. Although it might have been theoretically possible for Jesse to realize all of his aspirations, it was clear to me that he was still in the process of crystallizing his career identity.

Effective career decision making requires an element of dreaming about a variety of possible career futures. One of your career dreams might be a very unrealistic option. But there usually comes a time when it's important to shift from several unrealistic career goals to a few more realistic options.

Specifying

The second major developmental task of the exploration stage of career development is **specifying.** The specifying task of career exploration involves narrowing down possible career aspirations to a few options worthy of more detailed exploration.

Gabriella   CONSIDER

Consider the case of Gabriella, a 38-year-old woman whose youngest child recently entered kindergarten. After several years of enjoying a career as a homemaker and dabbling in various types of arts and crafts, Gabriella decided to return to college.

In order to help focus her time and make the best use of her money (this time *she* was paying for school!), Gabriella decided to spend a few months researching several careers that interested her.

Gabriella began the exploration process by looking into nursing, teaching, engineering, and court reporting as possible career choices. She also considered starting up a business of her own. It became apparent to Gabriella during this process that many of the careers she originally considered weren't very realistic options after all. Some (e.g., teaching and engineering) required more education than she was willing to complete. Others (e.g., court reporting and nursing) didn't allow her the flexibility that she was seeking in a new career. Gabriella was a prime example of someone working through the specifying task of career exploration.

Implementing

The third and final task of the exploration stage of career development involves **implementing** a career choice. As we begin to narrow career options and work toward making a tentative career choice, we need to strive for an increased understanding of our career self-concept. Taking into account our personality, interests, abilities, experiences, and values, coupled with an informed awareness of the world of work, we're equipped with the tools needed to make quality career decisions. Implementing a career choice means obtaining relevant education and/or training related to an occupation. It's an advanced phase of career exploration but *not* the end of it.

For an example of someone who is experiencing the early stages of implementing a career choice, let's return to the case of Gabriella. After narrowing down her list of potential career options during the specifying period of exploration, in the implementing phase Gabriella focused on careers that would allow her to fully implement her self-concept. She tried to figure out which career options fit best with her personality, abilities, interests, experiences, and values. Careful analysis of information Gabriella gathered helped her to conclude that starting up her own arts and crafts business was the best option to pursue. Gabriella attended small-business seminars, acquired skills associated with running a business, and even obtained a small-business loan from the government.

The majority of the chapters in this book focus on the exploration stage of career development. In each chapter, you'll learn how to integrate your self-concept, your knowledge about the world of work, and your understanding of employment opportunities to make the very best career decisions you possibly can.

Establishment

Once you've completed the exploration stage of career development, you'll enter the **establishment** stage, where you'll gain work experience associated with your career choice. It's a time for "trying out" your choice to determine if it's a good one.

CONSIDER   *Roberto*

Roberto, a student I worked with several years ago, was in the process of changing careers. After 15 years of working for the same company, Roberto decided that being a draftsperson wasn't as challenging or rewarding as it once was. After several months of career exploration, Roberto decided to pursue a career in radio broadcasting.

Roberto always had an interest in radio and even worked for a commercial radio station part-time during college. When it was time to declare a major, however, Roberto was afraid he might be discriminated against because of his Hispanic background when it came to finding a full-time job in the radio industry. He knew that the job market in radio was extremely tough to break into and he was well aware that few Hispanic people ever "made it" in broadcasting.

After Roberto and I talked about federal laws that prohibit discrimination on the basis of one's ethnic and cultural background, Roberto gained some of the confidence he needed to pursue his lifelong interest in radio. Soon thereafter he obtained a newscasting position at a local radio station. During the first few months on the job, Roberto gained a much better sense of what a career in radio broadcasting was all about. He learned about upward mobility possibilities within the industry, discovered what skills he needed to develop to succeed, and gained a clearer perspective about broadcasting careers in general.

During this initial employment phase, Roberto learned that he enjoyed broadcasting even more than he thought he would. Today, seven years later, Roberto is the general manager of one of the most popular radio stations in Los Angeles.

Maintenance

The fourth stage of the career development process is the **maintenance** stage, where stability within a particular career becomes the primary objective. Most persons in the maintenance stage continue to improve working conditions and experience growth and development within their chosen careers. Others, however, realize that they're in need of a different career altogether.

CONSIDER   *Darla*

Consider the case of Darla, a 33-year-old woman who came to my office one afternoon to discuss some of the problems she was facing in her current job. Darla was a regional sales manager for a large paper manufacturing company. Like many of her friends, Darla had majored in business during college. She recalled her reasons for making the decision to major in business. First, most labor projections that came out during Darla's college years indicated a large increase in business-related occupations. She enjoyed working with people and thought that business management would be a suitable career choice. Second, Darla had epilepsy and thought that a career in business would provide her with the type of work setting that wouldn't jeopardize her safety or the safety of others.

After eight years with the same company, Darla began to realize that continuing a career in business was not going to provide her with lasting satisfaction. In fact, she was worried that her performance on the job was slipping a bit because of her decreased interest in her career. She couldn't pinpoint exactly why the job was no longer as appealing as it once had been, although she identified the increase in paperwork and the decrease in interpersonal interactions as particularly disturbing. Furthermore, medications that had recently become available helped Darla gain increased control over her epilepsy, opening up a host of new career possibilities.

When Darla and I first met, she lacked some of the confidence she needed to begin the process of exploring a career change. However, after engaging in several months of self-reflection and researching information about the world of work, Darla decided to re-enter the exploration stage of career development and began thinking about new career options.

Disengagement

In the last stage of career development, **disengagement,** there is a reduction in the role that work plays in one's life. Individuals in the disengagement stage make a decision to retire or to change careers altogether. Keeping in mind that career decision making is a lifelong process, it's important to note that disengagement can occur several times throughout one's work history. Eventually the disengagement stage is a time when people retire from work altogether, but for many people disengagement represents a transition from one career to another. Darla eventually reached this stage as she completed career exploration activities and selected a new career as a high school teacher.

Remember, career decision making is a developmental process that varies from person to person. You may find yourself in the growth stage of development at the same time that one of your friends who's the same age you are seems to be pretty well established in a career and has moved on to the stage of maintenance. You might be experiencing disengagement from a career that you thought you'd be in until retirement. Perhaps you're now faced with the need to go back and reacquaint yourself with the world of work and begin the process of career exploration all over again. If so, don't despair. As mentioned earlier, recycling through the stages of career development is becoming more and more of a reality for almost everyone.

DETERMINING WHERE YOU ARE IN THE PROCESS

If you learn *how* to engage in effective career exploration, you'll master the tools needed for making good career decisions. Learning about the career decision-making process begins as you increase your self-understanding. Exercises 2.1, "Your Career Autobiography," and 2.2, "Identifying Your Career Needs," will assist you in determining where you are in the career decision-making process. Then, in Chapters 3 and 4, you'll complete several exercises that will assess your personality, interests, abilities, experiences, and values. Each of these exercises will increase

Learning how to engage in effective career exploration will give you the tools you'll need for making good career decisions.

your awareness of your self-concept as you prepare to embark on the important journey of career exploration and planning.

EXERCISE 2.1	*YOUR CAREER AUTOBIOGRAPHY*

This exercise is designed to assist you in discovering which of the five developmental stages of career decision making are the focus of your current life situation.

In the spaces provided on the next page, you're invited to write a brief, informal autobiography of experiences in your life that are relevant to your career development. You might begin by describing your career dreams, including occupations you have named in the past, when you were young, when someone asked you, "What do you want to be when you grow up?" Discuss how your career dreams have influenced some of the decisions you've made up to this point in your life.

Also be sure to list any jobs, volunteer work, or internships you've had. Explain how these experiences provided you with information about your interests and skills. Hobbies, leisure activities, and athletic participation also should be included in your autobiography.

Be sure to mention any significant events in your life that have played a role in previous career decisions. Reflect upon the many ways that your cultural and ethnic background, socioeconomic status, gender, and religious beliefs have influenced your career decisions.

Finally, conclude your autobiography with a discussion of the various career issues you're facing today and strategies you plan to use to address these issues.

Before you actually begin to write your autobiography, take some time to think about what you want to include in it. You might even wait a couple of days before completing this exercise so that you can review some of the significant events in your

life. Self-reflection is especially important in this exercise.

Many students I've worked with claim that there isn't much for them to include in a career autobiography at this point in their lives. They mention that they've only held a couple of part-time jobs over the years and don't have any work experience worth mentioning.

Perhaps you find yourself in the same situation. If so, remember that even part-time work experiences are an important part of your career autobiography. The degree to which you've enjoyed any previous work experiences—whether full- or part-time—plays an important role in career decision making. *All* of your thoughts and feelings about making career decisions—whether seemingly insignificant or not—should be included in your autobiography.

Topics to consider as you prepare your autobiography include the following:

- Career dreams
- Previous paid employment experiences
- Volunteer experiences
- Internship activities
- Hobbies
- Leisure interests

- Athletic participation
- Ethnic background and heritage
- Socioeconomic status
- Gender roles
- Current educational status
- Current employment status
- Questions about your future
- Careers that seem interesting to you
- Career-related issues you're currently facing

Career Autobiography

_____

_____

_____

_____

_____

_____

_____

_____

_____

_____

_____

_____

_____

_____

_____

_____

_____

_____

_____

_____

_____

_____

_____

If you need more space, continue your autobiography on additional sheets of paper.

EXERCISE 2.2   *IDENTIFYING YOUR CAREER NEEDS*

(Make sure you've completed your Career Autobiography before proceeding with this exercise.)

By completing your autobiography, you've probably learned something about yourself and about your career development up to this point in your life. You can greatly increase your awareness of your self-concept by reflecting on past experiences.

To determine which developmental stage you're currently experiencing, go back to your autobiography and highlight (or draw a circle around) any information that describes your *current situation*. Although most of this material will probably be at the end of your autobiography, there may be reference to your current career status in earlier portions of your autobiography as well. *Any* information that explains issues you're facing or the decisions you're hoping to make in the near future should be highlighted in some way to signify its relevance to your current situation.

Now compare the information you've highlighted in your career autobiography with the chart in Table 2.1. Check the boxes that correspond with the stages of career development that you most directly identify with at this time. Once you've completed this exercise, you should have a pretty good idea of where you are in the career development process.

The far right column of the table suggests the career needs you're likely to be facing at this point in your career development, along with the chapters of this book that you'll find especially helpful in your current developmental stage.

TABLE 2.1   *Summary of career development stages.*

STAGE OF CAREER DEVELOPMENT	TYPES OF TASKS	SAMPLE AUTOBIOGRAPHY STATEMENTS	CAREER NEEDS
☐ Growth	(1) Forming work attitudes and behaviors	"I'm trying to figure out what I really want to do in life."	Learn about the world of work in general (Chapters 1 & 6)
	(2) Learning about the world of work	"I'm gathering lots of information about the job market."	Find out about trends in the labor market (Chapters 1 & 6)
			Get an idea of projections for some careers (Chapters 1 & 6)
			Increase self-understanding and awareness (Chapters 2–4)
			Determine your relevant interests and abilities (Chapter 3)
			Familiarize yourself with your work values (Chapter 4)
☐ Exploration	(1) Identifying career dreams	"I've always wanted to be a . . ."	Reflect on the careers you've dreamed about (Chapter 3)
	(2) Trying to narrow a list of career possibilities	"There are several occupations that interest me. I need to figure out which are realistic."	Develop a list of career options (Chapters 3, 4, & 5)
			Narrow your list to realistic options (Chapter 5)

(continued)

STAGE OF CAREER DEVELOPMENT	TYPES OF TASKS	SAMPLE AUTOBIOGRAPHY STATEMENTS	CAREER NEEDS
	(3) Determining your self-concept as it relates to the career decision-making process	"I'm not sure if I'll be really happy if I pursue *that* career."	Match your self-concept with a career choice (Chapter 5)
		"I'm wondering if it will be a career that I will enjoy for years to come."	Gather information about various careers (Chapters 5 & 6)
	(4) Deciding which career options to research	"Now I need to figure out which careers I need more information about."	Read about job trends for specific career areas (Chapter 6)
			Gather information about options you're pursuing (Chapter 6)
			Identify potential barriers to career success (Chapter 7)
			Learn ways to overcome barriers to success (Chapter 7)
			Identify support for decisions you're making (Chapter 7)
			Make a tentative career decision (Chapter 8)
			Set some clearly defined career choice goals (Chapter 9)
			Set up a timeline for realizing your goals (Chapter 9)
❏ Establishment	(1) Gaining work experiences related to your career choice	"I'm currently working in a job that will allow me the chance to see if I really want to pursue that career or not."	Continue the process of self-awareness (Chapters 3, 4, & 10)
	(2) Trying to determine the value of your choices	"Now that I'm working in this field, I'm not sure that my job is really meeting my needs."	Decide whether your values are being addressed (Chapter 4)
	(3) Continuing to increase self-understanding	"I'm learning a lot about myself as I continue to work in this field."	Set goals for gaining new experiences in an area (Chapter 9)
	(4) Beginning to stabilize within a career	"I'm satisfied with my current career."	Evaluate current job satisfaction (Appendix E)
❏ Maintenance	(1) Determining whether your current career situation is providing adequate satisfaction and fulfillment	"Lately I've been trying to determine whether I'm truly happy doing what I'm doing."	Determine whether to remain in a current job (Chapters 3–5)
		"I'm starting to think that maybe I should find out about other careers."	Evaluate current job satisfaction (Appendix E)
	(2) Searching for ways to increase job mobility	"Right now I'm trying to determine whether there is any chance that I might be promoted in the future."	Learn about other careers related to your job (Chapters 5 & 6)
	(3) Learning about other career options related to your current occupation	"I'm hoping that I will find some other jobs similar to my current one that I can consider applying for."	Learn about methods for locating new job opportunities (Appendix D)
❏ Disengagement	(1) Considering a new job or career change	"I'm pretty sure that I want to find a new job. This one is getting old."	Determine the appropriateness of a career change (Chapters 3–5; Appendix E)
	(2) Preparing for retirement	"I'm looking forward to golfing six days a week."	

As you can see, the main focus of this book is on the process of career exploration. So, now that you're aware of how the chapters that follow apply to your particular developmental stage, let the games begin!

SURFING THE WEB WITH A PURPOSE

www.ceap.wcu.edu/kirk/Course_Resources/career_dev/Super_careerdev_theory.html It's one of the longest Web site addresses I've ever seen, but it's worth typing into a browser! This site nicely summarizes Donald Super's career development theory, not only showing the five major stages of career development, but also discussing substages that fall within each major stage.

http://does.ci.washington.dc.us/careertheory.htm This site, sponsored by D. C. NetWorks, includes a nice summary of Super's career development theory. Also covered at this site are some other popular career theories, including John Holland's theory of careers.

http://ericacve.org/docs/genx.htm This brief article, written by Bettina A. Lankard and provided by the Educational Resources in Circulation (ERIC) Clearinghouse for Adult, Career, and Vocational Education, summarizes some of the challenging career development issues facing persons who fall into the "Generation X" population (born between 1960 and 1981).

www.cweb.com/inventory/ This address will take you to the Employment Search Readiness Inventory, part of the CareerWeb site. Completing the inventory will give you a better sense of where you are in the career exploration and planning process and how *Making Career Decisions That Count: A Practical Guide* can help you most.

QUESTIONS FOR CRITICAL THOUGHT

1. Why is career decision making considered a *developmental* process?
2. How can you learn more about your self-concept (i.e., your personality, interests, skills, experiences, and values) as it relates to making career choices?
3. What types of experiences are helpful for someone to have during the exploration stage of career development?
4. Why is it important to consider the educational and work-related experiences you've had as you begin the exploration stage of career decision making?

The pieces of the puzzle

ASSESSING YOUR PERSONALITY, INTERESTS, ABILITIES, & EXPERIENCES

Imagine completing all of your education and training without ever having to take a test. Although the thought of never taking tests may be appealing, you're probably aware why it is that we take tests. Simply put, tests provide us with the opportunity to measure our knowledge. Weekly spelling and vocabulary tests in elementary school, for example, assess how well we have mastered information presented to us in class. But tests aren't always given to people in order to grade them on their ability to recall specific information. Many tests, often referred to as **inventories** or **assessments,** are designed to help people learn more about who they are and what makes them different from everyone else.

As you may recall from Chapter 2, Dr. Donald Super's theory of career development emphasizes implementing as many parts of your self-concept as possible when making career decisions. In order for you to seek career choices that will provide you with the maximum opportunity to implement your self-concept, you first need to know what makes you who you are. The purpose of this chapter, and several chapters that follow, is to assist you in the process of increasing your awareness of your self-concept by examining your personality, interests, abilities, experiences, and values. Then you'll be prepared to make career decisions that will maximize your chances of success and satisfaction.

THE IMPORTANCE OF CAREER ASSESSMENT

LaTonya

A student I worked with several years ago, LaTonya, met with me to discuss some of her career concerns. She was attending a local university where she was about to complete her sophomore year, but she was having a difficult time deciding on a major. No matter how hard she tried, she wasn't able to figure out which major would be the best choice for her to make.

LaTonya had narrowed down her list of options to three different career fields, including careers in business, education, and social work. When I asked her how she had arrived at these particular options, she said that her choices had been based on advice from friends and family members. Her mother was encouraging LaTonya to go into business because of the money-making potential. Her father wanted her to become an elementary school teacher because he was confident that she would have a great time working with children. And LaTonya's friends were trying to convince her that she would be a great social worker because of her concern for others and her desire to help people.

I asked LaTonya what she was hoping to accomplish in her eventual career choice, and she had a rather difficult time explaining precisely what it was that *she*—independent from family members and friends—really wanted. I realized LaTonya hadn't engaged in an analysis of her own likes, dislikes, skills, and abilities, nor had she considered how some of her past experiences could help her make a better career decision.

LaTonya and I worked together for several weeks with the primary purpose of increasing her awareness of her self-concept. She completed several exercises, including assessments of personality, interests, skills, experiences, and values. Then we worked on searching for careers that maximized LaTonya's chances for implementing as many parts of her self-concept as possible. As it turned out, LaTonya was more interested in a career in public relations than in any of the careers her family and friends were encouraging her to consider.

Career counselors have long recognized the importance of assessing personality, interests, skills, experiences, and values when working with clients of all ages. It's not uncommon, for instance, for counselors to administer several different inventories or assessments to clients who seek their assistance. The results of such inventories often provide both the client and the counselor with important information to consider in the career decision-making process.

CONSIDER   *Gonzalo*

Whenever I think about the importance of assessment in career decision making, I'm usually reminded of Gonzalo, a student I worked with several years ago. Gonzalo was a 37-year-old electrical engineer employed as a shift supervisor at a large engineering firm in the Southwest. After 13 years at the same company, even though he had received promotions over the years, Gonzalo was no longer as satisfied with his career as he had once been.

I asked Gonzalo why this was so, and he explained that while he still enjoyed the emphasis on math and science that a career as an electrical engineer provided, he didn't enjoy working in a supervisory role, and the work wasn't fun any more.

Gonzalo told me about a new interest he had developed: working with adolescents. Gonzalo had volunteered to serve as a Cub Scout leader in his community and had discovered that he thoroughly enjoyed working with youth. As a result, Gonzalo had also volunteered to coach a soccer team, and he looked into the possibility of increasing his involvement in other youth activities in the community. Apparently, Gonzalo had developed an interest in working with adolescents but was unable to find an easy way to integrate that new interest into his work environment.

Gonzalo completed several personality, interest, and skills inventories that helped him make the eventual decision to pursue a career teaching high school math and coaching. Gonzalo might never have considered a career in education if he hadn't been willing to invest the time and energy necessary to re-evaluate his self-concept. The career assessment results verified his interests and abilities in working with adolescents.

Our interests aren't the only aspects of ourselves that change: our job-related abilities and experiences, as well as our values, also change over time. That's why periodic assessments of all aspects of our self-concept—our personality, interests, abilities, experiences, *and* values—can be so important when we're making career decisions.

ASSESSMENT OF PERSONALITY

One of the best ways to begin the process of gathering information about yourself is to consider your personality. Your **personality** is your way of perceiving the world and the things that happen to you. It's the way you generally tend to handle things. As you may already know, psychologists have discovered that our personalities are influential in the development of our attitudes and behavior.

One way to learn more about your personality is to complete a personality or temperament inventory. One of the most popular measures of personality used to help students make career decisions is the Myers-Briggs Type Indicator®, commonly referred to as the MBTI. If you have the chance to complete the MBTI, you'll probably want to take advantage of that opportunity. Learning more about your personality type will help you increase your awareness of your self-concept.

The MBTI is based on a theory of psychological types developed by Dr. Carl Jung. According to Dr. Jung, there are four different personality dimensions that interact with one another to determine a person's psychological type. These four dimensions of personality are briefly described in the box below.

Your particular personality or psychological type is determined by combining your preferences in each of these four dimensions. For example, if you're the type of person who focuses your perception and judgments primarily on the external world of actions, objects, and persons (Extraversion), perceives information primarily in terms of meanings, concepts, and relationships (Intuition), makes judgments on the basis of personal, social, and subjective values (Feeling), and prefers flexibility, openness, and a free flow of information when dealing with the external world (Perception), then your psychological type would be characterized as Extraversion-Intuition-Feeling-Perception, or ENFP for short.

Your personality is your way of perceiving the world and the things that happen to you.

Four Dimensions of Personality

EXTRAVERSION vs. INTROVERSION

(E) Extraversion: Focusing your perceptions and judgments about things based on the external world of actions, objects, and persons

(I) Introversion: Focusing your perceptions and judgments about things based on the internal world of concepts and ideas

SENSING vs. INTUITION

(S) Sensing: Perceiving information primarily in terms of concrete facts and details

(N) Intuition: Perceiving information primarily in terms of meanings, concepts, and relationships

THINKING vs. FEELING

(T) Thinking: Making judgments and decisions primarily on the basis of logic and objective analysis

(F) Feeling: Making judgments and decisions primarily on the basis of personal, social, and subjective values

JUDGMENT vs. PERCEPTION

(J) Judgment: Preferring order, closure, and structure when dealing with others

(P) Perception: Preferring flexibility, openness, and a free flow of information when dealing with others

The developers of personality assessment instruments have found that certain types of work environments and careers are more attractive to persons of certain personality types. This can be valuable information for individuals exploring career options.

Exercise 3.1 will allow you to learn more about your personality and show you how this information about yourself can help you make a satisfying career choice.

EXERCISE 3.1   *WHAT'S MY TYPE?*

Step I.

For each of the following pairs of statements, check the option that describes you best. You *must* select one of the statements in each pair. There are no right or wrong answers.

SECTION ONE

_____ 1. I like to be around other people.

_____ I prefer spending time alone.

_____ 2. I prefer working on team projects.

_____ I'd rather complete a project on my own.

_____ 3. I often ask others for their opinions about decisions I have to make.

_____ I usually make important decisions on my own.

SECTION TWO

_____ 4. I like work that involves precise objectives and clearly defined details.

_____ I prefer work that is less defined and that requires very little precision.

_____ 5. I enjoy routine in the workplace.

_____ I dislike doing the same tasks at work every day.

_____ 6. I don't rely too much on inspiration when I'm involved in a project.

_____ Inspiration plays an important role in my work.

SECTION THREE

_____ 7. Most of the decisions I make at work are based on rational thinking and an analysis of the situation.

_____ I tend to make decisions at work based on what feels right to me at the time.

_____ 8. I don't usually focus too much on others' feelings about decisions that I make at work.

_____ I am usually very aware of others' feelings about decisions that I make at work.

_____ 9. I'm not too concerned about pleasing other people in the workplace.

_____ I enjoy making others feel good about themselves at work.

SECTION FOUR

_____10. I like making definite plans about my future.

_____ I prefer leaving my options open regarding future plans.

_____11. I like making well-defined decisions about things.

_____ I don't like making definite decisions about things.

_____12. I prefer rigid, clear-cut direc-   _____ I'd rather work on a task that's
tions when working on a task.   less clearly defined and allows
                                                for flexibility and change.

Step II. Scoring

As you may have figured out while completing Step I of this exercise, each section
represents a different personality dimension. Section One statements reflect the
Extraversion vs. Introversion dimension of personality. The statements on the left
side represent Extraversion, whereas the statements on the right side represent
Introversion. Section Two statements represent the Sensing vs. Intuition dimension, with statements on the left side reflecting a Sensing orientation and
statements on the right side reflecting an Intuition orientation. Section Three
statements represent Thinking (statements on the left side) vs. Feeling (statements
on the right side), and Section Four statements reflect Judgment (left side) vs.
Perception (right side).

   To get a rough estimate of your personality type (realizing that your true psychological type can only be reliably assessed by a lengthier assessment, such as the
MBTI), determine which personality orientation in each section you tend to
associate with by figuring out which types of statements you marked as describing you best. If, for example, you checked off two statements on the left side of
Section One and only one statement on the right side, or all three statements on
the left side, then you probably have Extraversion (E) dominance on that particular dimension.

   Indicate below your preferences based on your analysis of preferences in each
domain:

SECTION ONE

   Extraversion (E) _____   Introversion (I) _____

SECTION TWO

   Sensing (S)   _____   Intuition (N)   _____

SECTION THREE

   Thinking (T)   _____   Feeling (F)   _____

SECTION FOUR

   Judgment (J)   _____   Perception (P) _____

Now place the letter of your preference in each dimension (in order) in the spaces
below:

   Your Type: _____ _____ _____ _____
   Section   1   2   3   4

Step III. Careers and Personality Type

Developers of personality assessment instruments have found that certain types of
work environments and careers are more attractive to some people than they are to
others, depending on personality type. Persons who identify more with Extraversion
than Introversion, for example, are probably going to be much more satisfied in a
career that involves a lot of opportunity to work with others in a group or team setting. On the other hand, individuals with an Introversion orientation are probably
much more satisfied in careers that maximize opportunities to work alone or in one-
on-one situations.

Sensing individuals usually like careers that involve concrete facts and data, whereas intuitive types probably find careers with less structure and detail much more rewarding. As you might imagine, individuals with a thinking orientation prefer careers that involve logical reasoning, whereas individuals with a feeling orientation prefer careers that involve feelings and emotions. Finally, it follows that persons who possess a judgment orientation enjoy careers with a high degree of organization, structure, and routine, whereas persons who possess a perceiving orientation prefer careers with a high degree of flexibility and spontaneity.

In his book *Introduction to Type and Career*, Allen Hammer put together a list of specific careers that persons with certain psychological types often find most attractive. This list can be found in Appendix A at the back of this book. As you look through the list of occupations that match your psychological type, don't be surprised if a few of the occupations don't seem to fit your personality perfectly. Even though you share many aspects of your personality with other people who share your psychological type, you're not necessarily going to prefer *all* of the careers that are generally attractive to folks with that type.

List below any of the careers under your psychological type in Appendix A that seem interesting to you. If you've had the opportunity to complete the MBTI, include any occupations generated from the actual MBTI report that you'd like to explore.

We'll be taking another look at the importance of your personality and the careers you've listed above later on in the career exploration and planning process.

ASSESSMENT OF INTERESTS

The most commonly administered career assessments are interest inventories. These types of assessments include popular measures such as the Self-Directed Search, the Strong Interest Inventory, and the Kuder Career Search with Person Match. Interest inventories are designed to help people think about their interests in a variety of leisure activities, academic areas, and work environments. An individual's particular interests are then compared to the interests of other persons who have completed the inventory and who are satisfied with their career choice.

Interest inventories help people think about interests in leisure activities, academic areas, and work environments.

Say, for example, that a first-year college student named Stacia completes the on-line version of the Kuder Career Search (KCS) with Person Match™ by logging on to www.kuder.com. After she completes the inventory, it is immediately scored on-line. During the scoring process, Stacia's responses to the various items on the inventory are compared to the answers provided by persons representing hundreds of different occupations who completed the very same inventory. This comparison group is comprised of workers who report a very high level of satisfaction with their career.

If Stacia's responses to the KCS with Person Match™ are similar to the responses provided by an accountant, then the inventory's on-line interpretive report for Stacia will suggest that she consider exploring a career in accounting. If, on the other hand, Stacia's responses differ greatly from the responses provided by the accountant, then the report would *not* suggest accounting as a possible career field of interest.

As you might imagine, results from interest inventories can provide you with helpful information in making some initial career decisions. By learning which career areas are compatible with your interests, you can explore specific opportunities that exist within those particular areas. Exercise 3.2, Career Dreaming, and Exercise 3.3, Activities Ratings, will provide you with the type of increased awareness of your interests that will help you throughout the career decision-making process.

CAREER DREAMING	**EXERCISE 3.2**

As you may recall from Chapter 2, Dr. Super used the term *crystallizing* to refer to some of the career decisions we often make when we're at the beginning of the career exploration process. I can remember being seven or eight years old and telling everyone that I was going to be a dentist when I grew up. I was simply fantasizing about a career that I found interesting at the time. Even at a very young age, most people have at least some idea of what they like and dislike, even though many of us eventually select careers that are very different from our early career fantasies.

This exercise gives you the chance to fantasize again, to consider those careers that you would pursue if there were no barriers whatsoever to prevent you from doing so. It's time to dream again! Forget for a moment about all of the reasons you shouldn't pursue a career you've found appealing. Instead, allow yourself to dream about the careers you'd "go for" if there were *no reasons at all* to stop you from doing so. List your career dreams in the spaces below:

CAREER DREAMS

1. _____
2. _____
3. _____
4. _____
5. _____
6. _____
7. _____
8. _____
9. _____
10. _____

You'll return to this exercise in Chapter 5 as you begin to integrate the results of several career assessments. In the meantime, if you think of any other career "dreams" in the next few days, be sure to add them to this list.

EXERCISE 3.3   *ACTIVITIES RATINGS*

To complete this exercise, simply rate your interest in each of the following activities. Use the scale shown below to rate your interest:

1	2	3	4	5
not interested at all	*not very interested*	*neutral*	*somewhat interested*	*very interested*

RATING	ACTIVITY
_____	1. Visiting a science museum
_____	2. Attending a seminar on public relations
_____	3. Developing an annual schedule of important events
_____	4. Discussing a philosophical concept or idea
_____	5. Enforcing a safety rule or procedure
_____	6. Camping in the mountains
_____	7. Conducting a science experiment
_____	8. Training adults in first aid techniques
_____	9. Writing a short story
_____	10. Participating in an outdoor activity
_____	11. Reviewing financial records
_____	12. Selling a new product
_____	13. Learning about local history
_____	14. Filing important documents
_____	15. Repairing a broken appliance
_____	16. Planting seeds in a garden
_____	17. Reading about recent scientific discoveries
_____	18. Organizing information gathered from "surfing" the Internet
_____	19. Teaching a subject you enjoy to a group of people
_____	20. Solving complex mathematical problems

RATING	ACTIVITY
_____	21. Operating large machinery
_____	22. Recording important details from a conversation
_____	23. Playing a musical instrument
_____	24. Marketing a new service to the public
_____	25. Diagnosing someone's illness
_____	26. Working with disadvantaged youth
_____	27. Rebuilding an engine
_____	28. Painting a picture of a landscape
_____	29. Talking to a group of people about legal matters
_____	30. Working on a farm
_____	31. Participating in an athletic event
_____	32. Working for a social service agency
_____	33. Selling real estate
_____	34. Auditioning for a musical or play
_____	35. Repairing a broken radio
_____	36. Reading the *Wall Street Journal*
_____	37. Watching a Supreme Court hearing
_____	38. Going to the zoo
_____	39. Taking a psychology or human relations course
_____	40. Fixing a broken computer

As with the other exercises in this chapter, we'll be scoring and integrating the results of this exercise when we get to Chapter 5.

ASSESSMENTS OF ABILITIES AND EXPERIENCES

In addition to personality and interest inventories, skills and experience assessments also are useful career decision-making tools. These types of inventories are designed to evaluate an individual's abilities in several different work-related domains. Some of these assessments are self-ratings of skill and involve nothing more than rating how good you *think* you are at certain work-related tasks. Other assessments, such as the Armed Services Vocational Aptitude Battery (ASVAB) and the Differential Aptitude Test (DAT), involve a detailed analysis of demonstrated work-related skills and abilities.

Career counselors will sometimes suggest that students complete a battery of ability tests to gather information about relevant work-related skills. The resulting information can help you figure out the practicality of various career options, thereby suggesting specific careers that you may not have otherwise considered.

Shelley   CONSIDER

Consider the case of Shelley, a sophomore I counseled while she was attending a large university in Southern California. Shelley took college very seriously. Her family was unable to help her financially, so she had to work 30 hours a week while going to college. She wanted to be very organized in her career planning, so she wasted no time beginning the process of career exploration.

Shelley was fairly sure that she wanted to pursue a career in either medicine or law, but she was having a difficult time deciding. She met with me for some guidance and direction about where to start the process of making a choice. When I asked Shelley how she had developed an interest in medicine and law, she described the series of personality and interest inventories (which included the MBTI, Self Directed Search, and the Strong Interest Inventory) that she had completed during her first year in college. The results of the inventories consistently revealed that careers in medicine and law were directly related to her hobbies and interests. Shelley was especially attracted to professions that would provide her the opportunity to help others, and she was confident after interviewing various doctors and lawyers that either profession would be rewarding.

Until our work together, however, Shelley didn't have a really clear sense of her specific skills associated with law and medicine. Most of the classes she had completed during her first year were general education courses. Although she enjoyed most of her first-year classes, they didn't provide her with the chance to explore her abilities in areas directly related to medicine and law. We agreed that completion of an aptitude assessment would be helpful.

Shelly agreed to take the DAT, an aptitude battery designed to measure a person's ability to learn or to succeed in certain work-related areas. Results of the DAT indicated that Shelley possessed many of the skills associated with a career in medicine. She scored exceptionally high on the Numerical Reasoning and Abstract Reasoning scales, providing evidence of her math and science ability and her ability to solve complex problems.

Although Shelley possessed many of the skills related to a career in law, as revealed by her moderately high scores on the Verbal Reasoning and Language Use scales, she demonstrated somewhat lower skills in many of these areas relative to her performance in the domains related to a career in medicine. Our discussions also revealed that Shelley was less confident in her ability to engage in oral arguments and debate than in her ability to diagnose problems and work on investigative tasks. The information about Shelley's skills and abilities that we gathered from the assessments, along with other discussions we had, helped her make the eventual decision to enroll in the college's pre-med program.

As you engage in the process of making career decisions, it will be helpful for you to assess your strengths and weaknesses and learn to integrate that information into your career choice. As with assessments of personality and interests, if you

have access to a reliable and valid assessment of skills and abilities, you should consider completing such an assessment. Exercise 3.4, "Linking the Past to the Present," and Exercise 3.5, "How Well Do You Do What You Do?," will help you begin to think about the ways that past experiences have helped you acquire various work-related skills.

EXERCISE 3.4   *LINKING THE PAST TO THE PRESENT*

To complete this exercise, simply evaluate how much experience you've had with each of the activities listed below. There may be some activities that you've not yet experienced, but you probably have at least some experience with most. Use the scale below when rating your experience with each of the following activities.

1	2	3	4	5
no experience at all	very little experience	moderate experience	very much experience	lots and lots of experience

RATING	ACTIVITY
_____	1. Creating artwork
_____	2. Serving other people
_____	3. Promoting new products or services
_____	4. Hiking in the mountains
_____	5. Solving mathematical problems
_____	6. Working with tools to fix things
_____	7. Managing other people's work
_____	8. Teaching children how to read
_____	9. Playing musical instruments
_____	10. Participating in volunteer work
_____	11. Conducting research studies
_____	12. Planting vegetables in a garden
_____	13. Selling things to customers
_____	14. Drawing or sketching pictures
_____	15. Hunting and/or fishing
_____	16. Debating a political topic
_____	17. Finding answers to legal questions
_____	18. Reading science books
_____	19. Entertaining people
_____	20. Discussing business principles and concepts
_____	21. Repairing broken machines or equipment

RATING	ACTIVITY
_____	22. Collecting scientific data
_____	23. Selling insurance
_____	24. Organizing information into a word-processing document
_____	25. Helping people work through their personal problems
_____	26. Rebuilding an engine or appliance
_____	27. Pondering the meaning of life
_____	28. Convincing people to purchase a particular brand or product
_____	29. Filing important documents
_____	30. Working outdoors
_____	31. Writing a news story
_____	32. Finding answers to medical questions
_____	33. Decorating rooms in a house
_____	34. Building things from scratch
_____	35. Doing your taxes
_____	36. Helping someone figure out which career to pursue
_____	37. Selling cars
_____	38. Designing a new home
_____	39. Harvesting crops
_____	40. Reading about your local town's history

HOW WELL DO YOU DO WHAT YOU DO?　　　　EXERCISE 3.5

To complete this exercise, indicate your skill level for each of the activities listed below. Use the following scale for rating your skills:

1	2	3	4	5
no skill at all	*very little skill*	*moderate skill*	*high skill*	*very high skill*

RATING	ACTIVITY
_____	1. Tutoring others in a subject you're good at
_____	2. Working with animals/livestock
_____	3. Understanding a complex legal argument
_____	4. Managing people to accomplish a particular task
_____	5. Promoting a new product
_____	6. Creating a work of art
_____	7. Understanding the meaning of philosophical ideas or concepts
_____	8. Operating farm machinery
_____	9. Using a word-processing program
_____	10. Fixing broken machines
_____	11. Designing the interior of a house
_____	12. Solving mathematical problems
_____	13. Developing new friendships
_____	14. Playing musical instruments
_____	15. Convincing someone to buy a particular brand or product
_____	16. Influencing people to agree with your ideas
_____	17. Understanding others' feelings
_____	18. Describing how a machine works
_____	19. Teaching people to complete a difficult task
_____	20. Managing a database of information
_____	21. Finding solutions to scientific problems

RATING	ACTIVITY
_____	22. Presenting a public presentation on a current event topic
_____	23. Showing compassion to others
_____	24. Maintaining a garden of fruits and vegetables
_____	25. Selling automobile and/or life insurance
_____	26. Working for a construction company building homes
_____	27. Researching the causes of a medical illness or disease
_____	28. Accurately proofreading an essay
_____	29. Developing an organized method of running an office
_____	30. Handling emergency situations
_____	31. Landscaping the front yard of a new home
_____	32. Understanding a scientific explanation of something
_____	33. Reassembling an appliance after fixing it
_____	34. Engaging in competitive athletic events
_____	35. Working as a retail salesperson
_____	36. Researching a scientific topic on the Internet
_____	37. Building kitchen cabinets for a new house
_____	38. Owning and/or operating a farm
_____	39. Developing a marketing plan to sell a new product
_____	40. Performing in front of a large audience

When we get to Chapter 5, we'll score and interpret the results of this and the other exercises in the chapter. But first you'll need to explore your values and gain a better understanding of how your values influence your career decisions. This is the focus of Chapter 4.

OTHER TYPES OF CAREER ASSESSMENT

In addition to personality and interest inventories and measures of experiences and skills, test developers have created many other assessments to help us make well-informed career decisions. You may want to meet with a career counselor to find out what career assessments are available to you.

Career counselors are professional counselors who specialize in helping people in all aspects of the career decision-making process. Most career counselors have master's or doctoral degrees in counseling and have completed several years of professional training. You might find it very helpful to seek the assistance of a career counselor and participate in a thorough evaluation of your personality, interests, skills, and values.

Remember that career assessments are helpful because they increase our understanding of ourselves. Most of us already have a pretty good idea of who we are, but we don't often think all that much about our personality, interests, skills, and values as they relate to making career decisions. That's where meeting with a career counselor can help. Check with your college or university career planning and/or counseling center to see if career-counseling services are available to you. If not, a quick look through the yellow pages will probably reveal a listing of private career counselors who provide services in your area.

Career counselors specialize in helping people in all aspects of the career development process.

SURFING THE WEB WITH A PURPOSE

www.keirsey.com/contents.html This site allows you to complete the Keirsey Temperament Sorter (in any of seven different languages) without any charge to you. You can use your results on this inventory to determine your Myers-Briggs personality type.

http://cbweb9p.collegeboard.org/career/html/searchQues.html This inventory, developed by the College Board, is a career questionnaire that assesses your interests and abilities by asking questions that fall into various categories: Temperaments, Abilities, Working Conditions, Education, Interest Areas, Salary Requirements, and Employment Outlook. Upon completing the questionnaire, your responses are scored and you receive a brief report.

www.psychometrics.com/scales/tstart.htm This site, copyrighted by Lionel Arsenaul and Psychometrics Canada Ltd., provides you with the opportunity to complete the TRIMA Career Competency Questionnaire. The questionnaire consists of 150 questions and takes about 15 minutes to complete. As with most on-line assessments, your responses are immediately scored and interpreted for you.

www.queendom.com/test_frm.html Although they may not be as reliable or valid as many other assessments that are available on the Web, the numerous assessment links that you'll find at this site will take you to a variety of career/job assessments, including assessments that measure coping skills, time management, leadership, assertiveness, and personality type.

QUESTIONS FOR CRITICAL THOUGHT

1. How does your personality influence your beliefs and actions?
2. Why is it important for you to identify your career "dreams"?
3. Why shouldn't you base your career decisions solely on what you like to do?
4. How do experiences you had as a child and adolescent influence your career decisions as an adult?

What matters most?

RECOGNIZING THE IMPORTANCE OF YOUR VALUES

J ust as assessments of our personality, interests, experiences, and abilities are important in the process of making career decisions, equally important are assessments of our values. Making a career decision based only on what we like and what we're good at can lead to job dissatisfaction and unhappiness. Why? Because knowing about our own personal values and understanding how those values influence our happiness and satisfaction are critical to making good career decisions.

As you begin to consider various career possibilities, you'll be sure to benefit from a thorough evaluation of your values. The purpose of this chapter is to introduce you to the role that values play in career decision making and to provide you with the opportunity to consider how your own personal values can be integrated into your career decision making.

THE ROLE OF WORK-RELATED VALUES

Over the past several years there have been many political discussions about values, including everything from the importance of family values to the ways that morality is depicted in the media. When we talk about values, it's helpful to recognize the many different ways values can be defined. Some of us think of values as morals or ethics. Others consider values to be important beliefs and opinions. A friend of mine defines values as those beliefs that are such an important part of who you are that you'd be willing to die for them! This may sound like a pretty strong definition. But such a definition helps us realize why it's so important to consider values in career exploration and planning.

| *Hai* | CONSIDER |

I worked with a student several years ago for whom this was especially true. Hai had made the decision to return to school after several years of working in a job he described as a "dead end." Long hours and lots of overtime week after week had taken their toll. Hai wanted to find a career that would allow him extra time to spend with his two children. Even though the financial security provided by his job was comforting, Hai felt like he had been neglecting his family.

Hai decided to enroll in night classes offered at the local community college. He wasn't sure of a particular career direction to follow, but he knew that he wanted a change. He recognized that by going back to school he'd be able to explore new careers and complete the necessary steps to make a career change possible.

Hai and I met so that I could assist him in the beginning stages of the career exploration process. Results of personality, interest, and ability tests he completed validated his thinking that a career in either a math- or science-related field would be appropriate. Hai had always enjoyed math and science classes in high school, and, although he hadn't ever attended college, he had always maintained his interest in science and math. He mentioned, for example, that he was an avid member of several computer clubs in his community. He also had developed a special interest in the Internet. He recalled that classes requiring some type of computer work were his favorites.

When we began to explore Hai's work-related values and how they had affected his career choices, I explained that values are like the cement that binds our career interests and skills together.

For two weeks, Hai engaged in a thorough evaluation of his values and began to realize that he valued job environments that maximized the opportunity for self-directed work activities. He also recognized that a job that allowed for creative expression corresponded with his work-related values.

After additional exploration, Hai decided to major in computer science. He began exploring career opportunities in private consulting as well as contract work in computer programming. Such options seemed to afford him the independence and freedom that he valued so highly.

Values are the cement that binds our career interests and skills together.

Work-related values, those things about our work environment that matter a great deal to us, are integrally connected with our on-the-job performance as well as our career-related satisfaction and success. Now is the time for you to begin to identify the work-related values you possess. Exercise 4.1, "What Makes Work Fun For You?," will help you with this process.

EXERCISE 4.1   *WHAT MAKES WORK FUN FOR YOU?*

A. Think about jobs you've had that you especially liked. What aspects of those jobs did you enjoy the most? Below is a list of work-related values associated with different types of careers. As you read through the list, decide which factors have contributed to your job satisfaction in the past or that you think will contribute to job satisfaction in the future. Remember to complete this exercise based on what work-related values *you* possess, not what values you *think* you should possess or what others (e.g., parents, siblings, friends) tell you that you should value.

Place a check mark next to the work-related factors listed below that you place a high value on:

_____   Salary

_____   Work location (indoors vs. outdoors)

_____   Benefits (e.g., health insurance, retirement plan)

_____   Stable employment

_____   Challenging work responsibilities

_____   Opportunities for advancement/promotion

_____   Opportunities to receive recognition for what you do

_____   Opportunities to develop new skills

_____   Opportunities for variety in your work

_____   Opportunities to travel

_____   Opportunities to work with tools and machines

_____   Opportunities to comfort other people

_____   Opportunities to educate or advise others

_____   Opportunities to be creative

_____   Opportunities to work independently

_____   Opportunities to encourage and motivate others

_____   Opportunities to engage in risk-taking, adventurous behavior

_____   Opportunities to supervise the work of others

_____   Opportunities to be systematic and organized in your work

_____   Opportunities to assist others less fortunate than you

_____   Opportunities to participate in innovative projects

_____   Opportunities to hold a position of high visibility

_____   Opportunities to work with other people

_____   Opportunities to influence or persuade others

_____   Opportunities to entertain others

B. The above list is far from comprehensive. List below any other aspects of the work environment that you highly value.

_____

_____

_____

_____

_____

_____

_____

C. Now rank the work-related values that you identified in Part A and the additional values listed in Part B *in the order of their importance to you.* Write in the value that is the most important to you on the first line below. On the second line, write in the item that is the second most important work-related value to you, and so on. Continue this process until you've listed all of those qualities that you checked off in Part A and included in Part B. The least important values will be toward the end of your list.

Most Important   _____

_____

_____

_____

_____

_____

_____

_____

_____

_____

_____

_____

Least Important   _____

We'll return to this list of work-related values later on in the career decision-making process.

CORE LIFE VALUES

When we talk about work-related values, we refer to aspects of the work environment that we experience on the job. Whether a particular occupation provides flexibility in work hours or the opportunity to interact with others or requires out-of-town travel: These are examples of the types of work-related characteristics that we need to examine when making career decisions.

As you continue with the career decision-making process you'll also need to consider other values you possess and how they influence your career satisfaction and success. I like to refer to these other, more personal values, as **core life values.** Core life values differ from work-related values in that they are all-encompassing. They represent the things in life that matter to you the most, the principles and beliefs that make you who you are.

Core life values are the principles and beliefs that make you who you are.

The best example I have to illustrate the importance of core life values in career decision making comes from my own experience as a student. Toward the end of my senior year in college, one of the decisions I had to make was whether to apply for graduate school. I was on my way to completing a bachelor's degree in psychology, and thoughts of entering a graduate program in counseling had crossed my mind. However, I was already employed on a part-time basis as a producer at a large radio station in Los Angeles, and for several years I had been set on pursuing a career in radio broadcasting.

I visited a career counselor, and we worked together for several weeks. I completed the MBTI and an interest inventory. Next we discussed my skills and abilities and talked about some of the experiences I enjoyed during high school and college. The results of the inventories and our discussions confirmed that both careers (radio broadcasting *and* counseling) seemed to be in line with my personality, interests, abilities, and experiences. I had a fair amount of interest in both options, I had demonstrated skills in both areas, and I had meaningful experiences in both.

I was beginning to think that I might as well toss a coin in the air to decide my career choice. That's when the counselor asked me to consider my values. I followed my counselor's advice and generated a list of core life values, those things that I strongly believe in and that matter to me more than anything else in life. I especially considered the role that my cultural background played in the development of my values. My Italian-American heritage and my middle class upbringing most definitely influenced my value system. I remember that the very first thing I put down on a sheet of paper later that night was the word "family." I went on to generate a list of seven or eight other core life values that matter a great deal to me, but it was that first one I listed, family, that had an all-important influence on my eventual career decision.

Because I took the time to consider those things in life that mattered to me most, I realized that a career as a counselor would provide much more flexibility than would a career in the entertainment industry and allow me ample time to attend to family relationships. The flexibility of work hours associated with operating a private counseling practice seemed much more in line with some of my core values than a career in radio broadcasting. It was the consideration of my values that helped me make a career decision that I've been extremely satisfied with ever since.

Personality, interests, abilities, and experiences are certainly important to consider in their own right, but gaining increased awareness of values and understanding their role in career development cannot be overlooked if you want to make career decisions that count. Exercise 4.2, "Getting at the Core: What Matters Most?," will help you identify some of your core life values.

GETTING AT THE CORE: WHAT MATTERS MOST?　　EXERCISE 4.2

In Exercise 4.1, we focused on work-related values, those values that are important to you in an actual career. Now we turn our attention to your core life values, those values that characterize what matters to you most in life.

Step 1. Begin by generating a list of the core values that you most strongly believe in. Allow yourself some time to think about the values that are most important to you. Be sure to consider the ways that your cultural and ethnic background, gender, age, and social class have influenced your value system.

Don't expect to be able to complete this exercise in a minute or two. The more thought you give to this exercise, the more successful you'll be at integrating your values into the career decision-making process. Remember, your core life values may not seem related to career decision making at all. That's okay, because you'll begin to see their relevance as you continue the exploration process.

To help you get started, the following core life values are provided to you as a reference. Feel free to include these and any other values that you consider to be important as you create your values list. Write those values that are most important to you on the "My Core Life Values List" that follows.

Achievement	Fame
Adventure	Family relationships
Availability to my children	Financial comfort
Availability to my spouse or significant other	Freedom
Church participation	Friendships
Community outreach	Generosity
Education	Health
Environment	Honesty
Ethics	Independence

Integrity   Recognition
Intellectual stimulation   Religion
Leisure time   Respect
Loyalty   Safety
Material wealth   Security
Patriotism   Sense of accomplishment
Personal appearance   Social status
Physical fitness   Spiritual development
Power   Time to myself

Step 2. Now consider what it is about each of the values included in your Core Life Values List that makes these values so important to you. Record your thoughts below.

My Core Life Values List

VALUE: _____

WHY IT IS IMPORTANT TO ME:

_____

_____

_____

_____

VALUE: _____

WHY IT IS IMPORTANT TO ME:

_____

_____

_____

_____

VALUE: _____

WHY IT IS IMPORTANT TO ME:

_____

_____

_____

_____

VALUE: _____

WHY IT IS IMPORTANT TO ME:

_____

_____

_____

_____

VALUE: _____

WHY IT IS IMPORTANT TO ME:

_____

_____

_____

_____

VALUE: _____

WHY IT IS IMPORTANT TO ME:

_____

_____

_____

_____

VALUE: _____

WHY IT IS IMPORTANT TO ME:

_____

_____

_____

_____

VALUE: _____

WHY IT IS IMPORTANT TO ME:

_____

_____

_____

_____

VALUE: _____

WHY IT IS IMPORTANT TO ME:

_____

_____

_____

_____

Step 3. Now rank order your core life values based on their relative importance to you. The value that is most important *to you* should be listed on the first line below, and the remainder of your core values should follow in order, just as in Exercise 4.1.

Most Important   _____

_____

_____

_____

_____

_____

_____

_____

_____

_____

_____

Least Important   _____

In Chapter 8 we'll discuss the ways your values can be integrated with information about your personality, interests, skills, and experiences to help you make career decisions that count.

SURFING THE WEB WITH A PURPOSE

www.wheaton.edu/CDC/plan/workvalu.htm Sponsored by Wheaton College Career Services, this site includes a list of more than 20 different work values that you might want to consider when developing your list of important work-related values.

http://career.berkeley.edu/Prep/PrepValues.stm This site, sponsored by the University of California, Berkeley, includes a list of 56 life values that go far beyond the traditional lists of work-related values. A rating scale is included to help you narrow down your list of core life values to the five or 10 that are most important to you.

http://web.bu.edu/counseling/careervalues.htm Sponsored by Boston University, this site discusses several values that many people consider to be important when seeking a career, including interest/stimulation, prestige, salary, time/work pace demands, work setting, and psychological/emotional needs.

www.nextsteps.org/net/career/81yecplc.htm The title of this site, Lifestyle Values, does a good job of summarizing what you'll find. In an evaluation of lifestyle values, you can rank and describe what each value means to you.

QUESTIONS FOR CRITICAL THOUGHT

1. Why is it important to consider your work-related and core life values when making career decisions?
2. What are some of the basic differences between work-related and core life values?
3. How did considering work-related values help Hai (one of Chapter 4's case studies) make a more informed career decision?
4. What types of work-related and core life values have you developed recently?

Making the pieces fit

This chapter will help you narrow your list of career possibilities to those that most closely match your personality, interests, abilities, experiences, and values. In many ways, this is the core chapter of the book. It is the chapter in which most of your hard work and dedication to the career decision-making process will begin to pay off. This chapter begins to tie together the information you've been gathering and the increased knowledge you now have about yourself as they relate to making a career decision.

In Chapter 1 you were introduced to the world of work and to some of the important issues you consider when making career decisions. If you followed some of Chapter 1's advice, then you've been storing information about different careers and the labor market in general.

In Chapter 2, you learned about Dr. Super's theory of career development and the five stages of the career decision-making process: growth, exploration, establishment, maintenance, and disengagement. In Chapters 3 and 4, we examined the importance of personality, interests, abilities, experiences, and values in career decision-making. You completed several assessments to increase your awareness of what makes you a unique individual.

Now that you've completed the exercises in Chapters 3 and 4, you're probably beginning to get a better sense of what Dr. Super meant by the term self-concept. Your own, personal understanding of who you are—of your likes and dislikes, your skills and weaknesses, your experiences and values—is what determines your self-concept. You are the best judge of what you enjoy doing and, as such, are the world's greatest expert when it comes to making your career decisions.

The purpose of this chapter is to help you begin to integrate information about your personality, interests, abilities, experiences, and values so that you'll be better prepared to make decisions about your future career. You'll learn how to evaluate your responses to the exercises in Chapter 3 as you begin to narrow your career possibilities. You'll also select four or five careers to explore in more depth in the chapters that follow.

MATCHING SELF-CONCEPTS WITH WORK ENVIRONMENTS

As you may recall from Chapter 1, Dr. Anne Roe categorized work environments according to eight different types: Service, Business Contact, Organization, Technology, Outdoors, Science, General Culture, and Arts and Entertainment. A summary of Dr. Roe's model is shown in Table 5.1.

Your job satisfaction, career stability, and on-the-job performance depend on the match between your self-concept and your work environment.

Like many other career counselors and vocational psychologists, Dr. Roe believed that our job satisfaction, career success, and on-the-job performance are directly related to the match between our self-concept and our work environment. Dr. John Holland, a world-renowned vocational psychologist referred to back in Chapter 1, calls this match **congruence.** Dr. Holland believes that individuals with high levels of congruence will be more satisfied with their careers, achieve greater success within their occupations, and will remain in their careers over a longer period of time. Persons with low levels of congruence, on the other hand, are likely to experience job dissatisfaction and relatively poor on-the-job performance. As a result, persons who are not in congruent work environments are likely to search for new and different employment opportunities (and sometimes new careers altogether).

| CONSIDER | *Chandra* |

To illustrate this concept let's turn to an example that I witnessed at the very beginning of my career. One of the first students I worked with was Chandra, a senior attending a college on the West Coast. Chandra was about to graduate with a degree in mechanical engineering. When I asked Chandra if she was excited to be graduating, she said rather emphatically, "No!" When I asked her to explain her answer, she talked about the many challenges she faced during college.

During her first year, Chandra found that she struggled a great deal when it came to writing assignments. She had a very hard time preparing research papers and found it

Summary of work environments. **TABLE 5.1**

WORK ENVIRONMENT	SAMPLE OCCUPATIONS	CHARACTERISTICS OF PEOPLE WHO LIKE WORKING IN THESE ENVIRONMENTS
Service	Social worker, Police officer, Family counselor, Occupational therapist	Enjoy serving and attending to the personal tastes, needs, and welfare of other people; obtain a strong sense of satisfaction from helping and/or protecting other people.
Business Contact	Real estate agent, Salesperson, Insurance agent, Public relations specialist	Enjoy persuading other people to engage in a particular course of action, such as the purchase of a commodity or service.
Organization	Employment manager, Human resources director, Business executive, Small-business owner	Enjoy engaging in tasks that involve a high level of organization and precision; often satisfied by supervising or managing others.
Technology	Repair Person, Mechanic, Civil engineer, Carpenter	Enjoy producing, transporting, and/or fixing things; more satisfied working with tools and objects than with people.
Outdoors	Forest Ranger, Horticulturalist, Wildlife specialist, Farmer	Enjoy working in outdoor settings; often favor working with animals and plants rather than with people.
Science	Chiropractor, X-ray technician, Dentist, Pediatrician	Enjoy working with scientific theory and its application to real-world problems.
General Culture	Lawyer, High school teacher, Librarian, Historian	Enjoy interacting with groups of people in an effort to preserve and/or transmit knowledge and cultural heritage.
Arts and Entertainment	Interior decorator, Artist Professional athlete, Actor	Enjoy environments that provide opportunities for artistic expression and/or the use of special skills in an entertainment industry.

extremely difficult to answer essay questions on tests. She just couldn't seem to get her thoughts down on paper very easily.

In her sophomore year Chandra discovered that she had a learning disability. After meeting with the Director of Special Student Services on campus, Chandra began to work though the challenges posed by her disability. She took advantage of the tutoring services available at the university and worked with her instructors to make sure appropriate accommodations were available in each of her classes. As a result, Chandra was able to overcome the challenges posed by her disability and performed very well in her more demanding engineering courses.

Despite the appearance that all was well, however, Chandra was not looking forward to graduation. She was anxious and fearful about beginning her career as an engineer. As we explored possible reasons for her feelings, it became apparent that Chandra's anxieties were due to one simple fact: she didn't like engineering! After four years of classes and even an internship in mechanical engineering, Chandra had come to realize that a career in engineering wasn't such a good choice after all.

As Chandra discussed her situation I was reminded of how important it is to engage in career exploration activities early on in college. I worked with Chandra to help her clarify the reasons why engineering wasn't as appealing as she thought it would be. I asked her to explain the work environment of an engineer to me. Then I asked her to describe the types of activities that she enjoyed, the range of abilities that she had, and the things that mattered most to her in life. It didn't take long for us to realize why a career in engineering wasn't all that appealing.

Chandra had been preparing for a career characterized in Dr. Roe's classification system as a Technical working environment. Mechanical engineers work with their hands a great deal, in a routine, organized setting with relatively little face-to-face contact with other people. Yet based on her self-concept (i.e., her understanding of her personality, her likes and interests, her skills and talents, and her values and beliefs), it was clear that Chandra was more Service oriented.

She loved to be around large groups of people. She enjoyed the opportunity to teach others and help them find solutions to their problems. She preferred working with people rather than with things, and she placed a high value on work that provided lots of opportunity to interact with others. For Chandra, a career as a mechanical engineer wasn't a very good match. A social service career would probably be much more fulfilling. Consequently, Chandra began to explore possible careers in fields such as social work and counseling.

The challenge is to seek career opportunities that will maximize your chances of establishing a high level of congruence between your career self-concept and your work environment, which brings us to the next stage in the process. It's time to integrate the results of the exercises you completed in Chapter 3. Doing so will help you identify work environments that are likely to provide you with job satisfaction, career stability, and on-the-job success.

For some people, brief descriptions of the eight work environments (such as those provided in Table 5.1) are all that's needed to identify careers likely to provide satisfaction, stability, and success. But assessments similar to those that you completed back in Chapters 3 and 4 provide additional information that almost always helps increase the overall effectiveness of a career decision.

As you complete the exercises in this chapter, you may find that the results of the Chapter 3 and Chapter 4 assessments validate a career choice you've already been considering. Or you may discover that the exercises helped you learn about aspects of yourself that you weren't aware of before. Either way, you're likely to discover that by completing these exercises you'll increase your awareness of your self-concept and enhance your ability to select the best type of work environment for *you*.

EXERCISE 5.1   *FINDING YOUR WORK ENVIRONMENT*

Begin by scoring the exercises that you completed in Chapter 3. To complete this process, remove Appendix B from the back of the book and follow the Scoring Directions.

For each of the Chapter 3 exercises that you score, you'll have a point value corresponding to each of the eight career types. Fill in those values in the spaces below.

Once you've recorded your scores for each exercise, compute your total scores for each career type by summing the scores for all five exercises.

SCORES FROM EXERCISE 3.1

Service	Business Contact	Organization	Technology	Outdoors	Science	General Culture	Arts & Entertainment
_____	_____	_____	_____	_____	_____	_____	_____

SCORES FROM EXERCISE 3.2

Service	Business Contact	Organization	Technology	Outdoors	Science	General Culture	Arts & Entertainment
_____	_____	_____	_____	_____	_____	_____	_____

SCORES FROM EXERCISE 3.3

Service	Business Contact	Organization	Technology	Outdoors	Science	General Culture	Arts & Entertainment
_____	_____	_____	_____	_____	_____	_____	_____

SCORES FROM EXERCISE 3.4

Service	Business Contact	Organization	Technology	Outdoors	Science	General Culture	Arts & Entertainment
_____	_____	_____	_____	_____	_____	_____	_____

SCORES FROM EXERCISE 3.5

Service	Business Contact	Organization	Technology	Outdoors	Science	General Culture	Arts & Entertainment
_____	_____	_____	_____	_____	_____	_____	_____

TOTAL SCORES (ADD THE SCORES IN THE COLUMNS ABOVE)

Service	Business Contact	Organization	Technology	Outdoors	Science	General Culture	Arts & Entertainment
_____	_____	_____	_____	_____	_____	_____	_____

Because the total scores are the combined results from the assessments you completed in Chapter 3, they include aspects of your personality, interests, skills, and experiences. The results can help you narrow your list of career possibilities.

Write in the three career types for which your total scores were the highest:

1. _____

2. _____

3. _____

Your primary "career type" is the category for which your score is the highest. Your secondary career type is the category for which your score is the second highest. Your third level of career type is the category for which your score is the third highest. If the scores for two of your types are identical, then your career type is probably best described as a combination of those two types.

IDENTIFYING CAREERS THAT MATCH YOUR CAREER TYPE

Now that you have a good idea what your primary career type is, it will be helpful for you to take a look at careers that are congruent with that type. You can begin this process by skimming through the career lists in Appendix C.

As you review the lists, make a note of those careers that pique your interest. Many of the careers listed in Appendix C may not be all that interesting to you, even though they correspond with your primary career type. That's actually very common. However, odds are that you'll find many of them rather interesting and, therefore, worthy of further exploration.

If your primary career type as revealed in Exercise 5.1 is several points higher than any of the other types, then you may want to focus your attention at this point on careers that correspond only with your primary type. If, however, the results of Exercise 5.1 revealed career types whose point totals were rather close to one another, then you might want to take a look at the careers listed in several of the career areas listed in Appendix C.

EXERCISE 5.2   *FINDING INTERESTING CAREERS FOR YOUR CAREER TYPE*

Make a list below of all careers that you're interested in pursuing further. Don't limit yourself only to those careers listed in Appendix C that correspond with your career type. Also consider other careers of interest to you, such as those listed on an interest inventory score report.

LIST OF INTERESTING CAREERS

_____

_____

_____

_____

_____

_____

_____

_____

_____

In order to complete some of the exercises that appear in the remaining chapters, you're going to need to narrow your list of potential career options to the four or five that interest you the most. For some folks, this is a rather easy task, but for others it can be a much more difficult enterprise.

CASE STUDIES IN NARROWING CAREER OPTIONS

CONSIDER   *Mario & Meredith*

Just as you've done in Chapter 3, Mario, a first-year college student, completed an interest inventory and a skills assessment. His results indicated that Mario possessed an Arts and Entertainment career type. He consulted Appendix C for a listing of occupations corresponding to the Arts and Entertainment work environment. Many of the careers in the list were ones that he had considered at different times throughout his life.

Mario knew he wanted to pursue a career that would involve creative expression as well as autonomy, but he also wanted a career that would provide a stable income. He had an actor friend who often went four or five months without work, and that simply wasn't something Mario was willing to do: he wanted the safety and security of a regular paycheck. Although his longer list of career possibilities included freelance artist and actor, Mario selected careers in interior design and commercial art to explore in more detail.

Meredith's situation was somewhat different from Mario's. She had a difficult time even generating a list of initial career options. Like Mario, Meredith had taken lots of different classes in college, but for Meredith none of them seemed to stand out as any more interesting than the others.

The results of Meredith's interest inventory and skills assessments helped her to understand why she was having such a difficult time narrowing down career options: her primary and secondary career types were nearly identical in value. When she completed Exercise 5.2, she discovered that Arts and Entertainment and Service career types were only two points different from one another. In essence, Meredith's career type was a combination of the two.

When it came time to look through lists of careers, Meredith took a look at both the Arts and Entertainment and Service occupation groupings. What resulted was a list of 18 occupations that she thought might be worth pursuing further. When I explained to her that she needed to narrow the list down to four or five, Meredith decided to consider the educational requirements associated with each career.

Meredith was a single mother with two children. She didn't want to select a career that would require several years of graduate school—at least not for now. That and her consideration of the earning potential of each career helped her to narrow down her options. Her resulting list of career possibilities included social worker, art teacher, and addictions counselor.

Whether your situation is more like Mario's or Meredith's, one thing is for sure: the information you've been gathering about the world of work and the increased awareness you have about your self-concept will help you a great deal as you narrow your list of potential careers down to four or five worthy of continued exploration.

Perhaps the most important things for you to keep in mind at this time are your work-related and core life values. As you begin to narrow your list of potential career options, it's very important that you think about pursuing careers that are congruent with your values. If you're like most people, you certainly don't want to engage in a thorough exploration of a career that's going to conflict with many of your work and life values. Before completing Exercise 5.3, "Narrowing Your Career Options," you should first review the values lists you generated back in Chapter 4.

Think about pursuing careers that are congruent with your values.

| NARROWING YOUR CAREER OPTIONS | EXERCISE 5.3 |

Based on the review of your values lists and the preliminary career choices you identified in Exercise 5.2 narrow your list of career possibilities to the four or five options that seem most worthy of continued exploration. Remember to think about the results of all of the research you've been engaging in. What have you learned about the world of work? How do your values seem supported or challenged by various careers? These are the kinds of questions you want to answer as you create your options list.

The time is now! List the four or five career options that you'd like to explore in more depth as you continue the career decision-making process.

CAREER OPTIONS TO EXPLORE FURTHER

1. _____

2. _____

3. _____

4. _____

5. _____

We'll refer back to this list in subsequent chapters as we discuss specific techniques for exploring career options.

SURFING THE WEB WITH A PURPOSE

www.bizjournals.com/atlanta/stories/1997/03/24/smallb3.html This site includes an article by Bob McDonald and Don Hutcheson that appeared in the *Atlanta Business Journal* in 1997. It is an excellent overview of the importance of seeking a good match between your natural abilities and interests and the career of your choice.

http://icpac.indiana.edu/infoseries/is-50.html The focus of this site is "discovering careers that fit you." After a brief discussion of John Holland's theory of careers, the site goes on to explain why knowing your abilities, assessing your skills, prioritizing your goals, and learning more about career opportunities is so important in the career exploration and planning process.

www.newwork.com/Pages/Opinion/McCracken/Holland.html Written by Dr. Dennis McCracken, this site provides a summary of John Holland's theory of careers and mentions several assessments and inventories that are available for purchase, for people who want to assess their vocational self-concept from Holland's perspective.

www.personal.ecu.edu/luciera.career.html This site includes a very well-written essay on sexual orientation and career decision making. Gay, lesbian, bisexual, and transgender persons will appreciate the author's efforts to identify issues that are particularly relevant to their experiences.

QUESTIONS FOR CRITICAL THOUGHT

1. What are some of the most important lessons you've learned about making career decisions from the first five chapters of the book?
2. Why do you suppose that *you* are the world's greatest expert when it comes to making *your* career decisions?
3. Why do you think that job satisfaction, career stability, and on-the-job success are all related to the degree to which your work environment and your career self-concept are congruent?
4. Why is it that so many adults end up working in environments that aren't congruent with their personality, interests, skills, or values?

Traveling through the maze

METHODS OF CAREER EXPLORATION

N ow that you've identified several careers you'd like to learn more about, it's time to actually engage in the process of fully researching these options to determine how congruent they are with your career self-concept. In this chapter, you'll learn various ways to determine which of the careers you're currently exploring are worthy of continued consideration. You'll be reminded of important concepts of career exploration presented earlier in the book. You'll also learn about several techniques for obtaining important employment-related information. The primary goal of this chapter is to assist you further in the process of narrowing down your list of potential career options as you prepare to make a tentative career decision.

A REVIEW OF THE CAREER EXPLORATION PROCESS

You may recall from Chapter 2 that Dr. Super referred to the second phase of the career decision-making process as exploration. In Chapters 3 and 4 you engaged in activities related to the crystallizing stage of exploration. You began by thinking about some of your career dreams and childhood aspirations.

Then you completed exercises designed to increase your understanding and awareness of your personality, interests, skills, experiences, and values. At the end of Chapter 5 you narrowed your original list of career options down to four or five to explore in more detail.

Now it's time to embark on the specifying sub-stage of career exploration. You'll make some critical decisions about whether to pursue a particular career or not. Each exercise completed during this stage of the career decision-making process will require you to do some important research about the careers you're exploring.

DEVELOPING AN ORGANIZED SYSTEM OF INFORMATION GATHERING

The first and most important activity that you'll engage in during this stage of career development is information gathering. In Chapter 1 you were encouraged to begin collecting and organizing materials from books, magazines, newspapers, and other sources that you might find particularly useful. You also were reminded about the information that student service groups, clubs, and organizations can provide.

Create a file for each of the occupations included in your "short list" of career possibilities.

If you haven't already done so, create a separate file for each of the occupations included in your "short list" of career possibilities. Throughout the next couple of weeks, you'll be collecting important information about these careers. An organized system for storing the information you collect will help you a great deal along the way.

GATHERING INFORMATION ABOUT CAREERS

Many resources are available to you for learning more about the careers you're exploring. This section describes each of these resources and explains why you should consider them in researching careers of interest.

You'll greatly benefit from getting to know your library's reference librarians and career center staff. Many of the resources you'll want to consult as you explore career options are available in public and college libraries and career centers. The more comfortable you are working with reference librarians and career center staff, the easier it will be to locate useful resources in your career search.

U. S. Department of Labor Publications
Occupational Outlook Handbook

As mentioned in Chapter 1, the *Occupational Outlook Handbook (OOH)* is published every two years by the U. S. Department of Labor's Bureau of Labor Statistics. Each issue of the handbook includes hundreds of occupations. For each one you will find a description of the nature of the work, general working conditions, expected earnings, educational and training qualifications, opportunities for advancement, and a five-year employment outlook. See Figure 6.1 for an example of an *OOH* entry.

The *OOH* also includes a listing of sources of additional information about a particular career. The *OOH* is available at most public libraries as well as college and university libraries and learning centers. Most campus-based career development and placement centers also keep a current copy on hand. Probably the most efficient way to use the *OOH* is to access the interactive on-line version at http://stats.bls.gov/ocohome.htm.

*O*NET*

O*NET, the Occupational Information Network, is an easy-to-use database that you can access with any Web browser. O*NET contains comprehensive information on job requirements and worker competencies for the most popular occupations. The information on O*NET (at www.doleta.gov/programs/onet) was developed by job analysts using a comprehensive structure based on skills. Future data that will appear on O*NET will come directly from workers and employers, describing the work they do, the skills they need, and the knowledge they use on the job.

Production Occupations

Assemblers

Precision Assemblers

(O*NET 87102C, 93102B, 93102C, 93102D, 93105, 93108, 93111A, 93111B, 93114, 93117, 93197A, and 93197C)

Significant Points

- Virtually all precision assemblers work in plants that manufacture durable goods.

- Most precision assemblers are promoted from the ranks of workers in lesser skilled jobs.

- Projected slower-than-average employment growth reflects increasing automation and the internationalization of production.

Nature of the Work

Precision assemblers are highly skilled workers who assemble a wide range of finished products from manufactured parts or subassemblies. They produce intricate manufactured products, such as aircraft, automobiles, computers, and small electrical and electronic components. Unlike some assemblers who perform simple, repetitive tasks, precision assemblers generally perform a series of more complex tasks.

Precision assemblers may work on subassemblies or the final assembly of finished products or components of an array of products. For example, precision electrical and electronic equipment assemblers put together or modify missile control systems, radio or test equipment, computers, machine-tool numerical controls, radar, sonar, and appliances, and prototypes of these and other products. Precision electromechanical equipment assemblers prepare and test equipment or devices such as dynamometers, ejection-seat mechanisms, and tape drives. Precision machine builders construct, assemble, or rebuild engines and turbines, and office, agricultural, construction, oil field, rolling mill, textile, woodworking, paper, printing, and food wrapping machinery. Precision aircraft assemblers put together and install parts of airplanes, space vehicles, or missiles, such as wings or landing gear. Precision structural metal fitters align and fit structural metal parts according to detailed specifications prior to welding or riveting.

Precision assemblers involved in product development read and interpret engineering specifications from text, drawings, and computer-aided drafting systems. They may also use a variety of tools and precision measuring instruments. Some experienced assemblers work with engineers and technicians, assembling prototypes or test products.

As technology changes, so too does the manufacturing process. For example, flexible manufacturing systems include the manufacturing applications of robotics, computers, programmable motion control, and various sensing technologies. These systems change the way goods are made, and affect the jobs of those who make them. The concept of cellular manufacturing, for example, places a greater premium on the communication and teamwork of "cells" than it does on the old assembly line process. As the U.S. manufacturing sector continues to evolve in the face of growing international competition and changing technology, the nature of precision assembly will change along with it.

Working Conditions

The working conditions for precision assemblers vary, from plant to plant and from industry to industry. Conditions may be noisy and many assemblers may have to sit or stand for long periods of time. Electronics assemblers, for example, sit at tables in rooms that are clean, well lit, and free from dust. Assemblers of aircraft and industrial machinery, however, usually come in contact with oil and grease, and their working areas may be quite noisy. They may also have to lift and fit heavy objects. In many cases, the increased use of robots or other pneumatically powered machinery has improved working conditions by lowering the overall noise level of the facility.

Most full-time assemblers work a 40-hour week, although overtime and shift work is fairly common in some industries. Work schedules of assemblers may vary at plants with more than one shift.

Employment

Virtually all of the 422,000 precision assembler jobs in 1998 were in plants that manufacture durable goods; 48 percent were electrical and electronic equipment assemblers. The distribution of employment among the various types of precision assemblers was as follows.

Precision assemblers produce intricate manufactured products such as small electrical and electronic components.

FIGURE 6.1 *Continued.*

444 Occupational Outlook Handbook

Electrical and electronic equipment assemblers	201,000
Machine builders and other precision machine assemblers	74,000
Electromechanical equipment assemblers	50,000
Fitters, structural metal	17,000
Aircraft assemblers	17,000
All other precision assemblers	64,000

Assembly of electronic and electrical machinery, equipment, and supplies, including electrical switches, welding equipment, electric motors, lighting equipment, household appliances, and radios and television sets accounted for 33 percent of all jobs. Industrial machinery assembly of diesel engines, steam turbine generators, farm tractors, mining and construction machinery, office machines, and the like accounted for 29 percent of all jobs. Other industries that employ many precision assemblers were transportation equipment (aircraft, autos, trucks, and buses) and instruments manufacturing.

The following list shows the wage and salary employment of precision assemblers in durable goods manufacturing in 1998 by industry.

Electronic and other electrical equipment manufacturing	137,000
Industrial machinery and equipment manufacturing	122,000
Transportation equipment manufacturing	63,000
Instruments and related products manufacturing	61,000
Fabricated metal products manufacturing	22,000
All other industries	2,200

Training, Other Qualifications, and Advancement

Most precision assemblers are promoted from the ranks of workers in lesser skilled jobs in the same establishment. The ability to do accurate work at a rapid pace is a key job requirement. A high school diploma is preferred.

Applicants need specialized training for some precision assembly jobs. For example, employers may require that applicants for electrical or electronic assembler jobs be technical school graduates or have equivalent military training. Some companies may also provide extensive on-the-job training or classroom instruction on the broad range of assembly duties that employees may be required to perform.

Good eyesight, with or without glasses, is required for assemblers who work with small parts. Plants that make electrical and electronic products may test applicants for color vision, because many of their products contain many differently colored wires. Manual dexterity and the ability to carry out complex, repetitive tasks quickly and methodically are also important.

As precision assemblers become more experienced, they may progress to jobs that require more skill and be given more responsibility. Experienced assemblers may become product repairers if they have learned the many assembly operations and understand the construction of a product. These workers fix assembled articles that operators or inspectors have identified as defective. Assemblers also can advance to quality control jobs or be promoted to supervisor. Experienced precision assemblers also may become members of research and development teams, working with engineers and other project designers to design, develop, and test new product models. In some companies, assemblers can become trainees for one of the skilled trades. Those with a background in math, science, and computers may advance to programmers or operators of more highly automated production equipment.

Job Outlook

Job growth among precision assemblers is expected to be slower than the average for all occupations through the year 2008, reflecting increasing automation and the internationalization of production. As manufacturers strive for greater precision and productivity, work that can be performed more economically or more efficiently by automated equipment will be transferred to these machines. In addition to jobs stemming from growth, many job openings will result from the need to replace workers transferring to other occupations or leaving the labor force.

Recent advancements have made robotics more applicable and more affordable in manufacturing. The introduction of robots should continue raising the productivity of assembly workers and adversely affecting their employment.

The effects of automation will be felt more acutely in some industries than in others. Flexible manufacturing systems are expensive, and a large volume of repetitive work is required to justify their purchase. Also, where the assembly parts involved are irregular in size or location, new technology is only now beginning to make inroads. For example, much precision assembly in the aerospace industry is done in hard-to-reach locations unsuited for robots—inside airplane fuselages or gear boxes, for example—and replacement of these workers by automated processes will be slower and less comprehensive than replacement of other workers such as welders and painters. On the other hand, automation will continue to make more inroads in the precision assembly of electronic goods, where a significant number of these workers are employed.

Many producers send their subassembly or component production functions to countries where labor costs are lower. This growing internationalization of production, promoted by more liberal trade and investment policies, results in shifts in the composition of this country's manufacturing workforce. For example, decisions by American corporations to relocate assembly in other nations may lead to employment reductions for precision assemblers in some industries. A freer trade environment will lead to growth in the export of goods assembled in the United States and will result in the creation of additional jobs in other industries.

Earnings

Earnings vary by industry, geographic region, skill, educational level, and complexity of the machinery operated. In 1998, median hourly earnings were $18.46 for aircraft assemblers, $12.59 for fitters, and $11.18 for electromechanical equipment assemblers.

Median hourly earnings of machine builders were $14.06 in 1998. The middle 50 percent earned between $11.11 and $17.24. The lowest 10 percent earned less than $9.02 and the highest 10 percent earned $21.29. Median hourly earnings in the manufacturing industries employing the largest numbers of machine builders in 1997 are shown below:

Motor vehicles	$16.60
Engines and turbines	14.80
Metalworking machinery	14.30
Construction and related machinery	13.50
Special industrial machinery	13.40
General industrial machinery	12.90

Median hourly earnings of electrical and electronic equipment assemblers were $10.45 in 1998. The middle 50 percent earned between $8.35 and $13.41. The lowest 10 percent earned less than $6.80 and the highest 10 percent earned more than $16.55. Median hourly earnings in the manufacturing industries employing the largest number of electrical and electronic equipment assemblers in 1997 are shown below:

Aircraft and parts	$13.40
Computer and office equipment	11.20
Search and navigation equipment	10.90
Communications equipment	9.90
Electronic components and accessories	8.70

Many precision assemblers are members of labor unions. These unions include the International Association of Machinists and Aerospace Workers; the United Electrical, Radio and Machine Workers of America; the United Automobile, Aerospace and Agricultural Implement Workers of America; the International Brotherhood of Electrical Workers; and the United Steelworkers of America.

Related Occupations

Other occupations that involve operating machines and tools and assembling products include welders, ophthalmic laboratory technicians, and machine operators.

Sources of Additional Information

Information about employment opportunities for assemblers is available from local offices of the State employment service and from locals of the unions mentioned earlier.

Occupational Outlook Quarterly

The U. S. Department of Labor's Bureau of Labor Statistics also publishes the *Occupational Outlook Quarterly (OOQ)*. This publication, which is arranged much like a magazine, serves as an update to the *OOH*. Each edition includes additional information about several of the jobs listed in the *OOH*. These quarterly updates can help you obtain the most accurate information available about most careers. The *OOQ* can usually be found at institutions that also have access to the *OOH*. An on-line version of the *OOQ* is available at http://stats.bls.gov/opub/ooq/ooqhome.htm.

Dictionary of Occupational Titles

The United States Government also publishes the *Dictionary of Occupational Titles* (DOT). Although somewhat outdated and expected to be altogether replaced in the near future by the O*NET system, the DOT can still be useful in its own right. It includes descriptions of thousands of occupational titles as well as a brief definition of each occupation and specific information about the skills required for successful performance within each occupation. The DOT also discusses the types of tasks and materials associated with each occupation, the industries with which the occupation is typically identified, and the working environment. Occupations are arranged alphabetically and by job categories. Like the OOH, the DOT is available at most libraries and college career centers. Some sites may have a computer software version available for your use as well. An Internet version can be found at www.oalj.dol.gov/libdot.htm.

Guide to Occupational Exploration

The *Guide to Occupational Exploration* can be a helpful source of information about particular careers you might be interested in. Originally developed as a supplement to the *DOT*, it includes details about various occupations arranged according to interest areas and work environments. The guide is not as widely available as the *OOH* or the *DOT*, but it may be worth seeking out, as it can provide you with data you can't find in other sources. If a *Guide for Occupational Exploration* is available to you, it would be worth your time and energy to look through it for useful information.

Additional U. S. Department of Labor Publications

In addition to publishing the *OOH*, the *OOQ*, the *DOT*, O*NET, and the *Guide for Occupational Exploration*, the U. S. Department of Labor also sponsors the publication of hundreds of other useful documents, such as "Job Options for Women" and the "Job Guide for Young Workers," to name a few. These and other publications that address particular aspects of the world of work are available at most local libraries. If you're unable to locate them, you can contact the Bureau of Labor Statistics, U. S. Department of Labor, Washington, DC 20212 (202-219-7316) or go to http://stats.bls.gov. The Bureau's Public Affairs Office will be able to help you obtain useful information relevant to the careers you're pursuing.

Encyclopedia of Careers and Vocational Guidance

The *Encyclopedia of Careers and Vocational Guidance* is similar in many ways to the *OOH*. The encyclopedia is published every few years by the J. G. Ferguson Publishing Company in Chicago and is found in the reference section of most libraries. The current edition of the *Encyclopedia* is published in four volumes, with separate volumes for industry profiles, professional careers, general and special careers, and technical careers. For each occupation, the *Encyclopedia* includes details about the history of the career, nature of the work involved, job requirements, employment opportunities, average salaries, and related occupations.

Magazines and General Trade Books

As briefly discussed back in Chapter 1, there are many magazines and general trade books that may help you locate information about careers of interest. Probably the best way to determine what information is available about a particular topic is to use an indexing system available at nearly every library. Most libraries these days provide electronic database searches for resources on a particular topic. By typing in a subject (e.g., "employment") or key terms (e.g., "downsizing" or "layoffs") you can receive a printout of available books, magazines, newspaper articles, and other media on the particular topic you're researching. The resource information is made available to you in a matter of seconds, saving you the time and energy that used to be required for a search through card catalogs and paper-based indexes.

There may be some magazines that you'll want to read on a regular basis so that you can get a good idea of general employment and labor trends. Magazines such as *Business Week, Forbes, Fortune,* and *Inc.* can be especially useful in this regard. As a rule of thumb, keep your eye out for *any* material that may help you gain a better understanding of the world of work and the occupations that interest you. Be sure to consult magazines and books that are especially relevant to your life situation. There are many magazines of particular relevance to persons of certain ethnic and racial backgrounds, to women, or to persons with disabilities.

Newspapers

Many of the newspapers with large circulations, such as the *Los Angeles Times* or the *Washington Post,* cover labor market and employment projections on a fairly regular basis. The *Wall Street Journal* is another reliable source of information about the world of work. However, as mentioned earlier, don't forget about your local newspaper. The most accurate information about local and regional trends in the job market is more likely to be found in your local newspaper than in any national or international publication.

College and University Career Centers

If you're currently attending college, don't forget to check out the services offered by your own institution. Most colleges and universities offer a wide variety of career exploration and planning services. In addition to carrying many of the resources discussed in this chapter, career development centers usually have established networks for linking you with community businesses that can be particularly valuable during your job search. Career counselors also can put you in touch with appropriate support services on campus that may assist you throughout the career exploration process.

Informational Videos

Videotapes can be another useful source of information about career possibilities. Individuals who are currently employed in various careers are often interviewed for documentary-type videos, which often provide important information about occupations. Informational videos can be especially helpful in giving you an idea of what job settings are like on a day-to-day basis. These types of videotapes are often available from career centers or school libraries.

Computerized Career Information and Guidance Programs

One of the best ways to locate information about occupations is to learn about and use computerized career information and guidance programs available in most college and university career centers. The more popular programs include the System of Interactive Guidance and Information (SIGIplus), Computerized Heuristic Occupational Information and Career Exploration System (CHOICES), DISCOVER, and Career Information System (CIS).

Computerized career information and guidance systems can provide you with both up-to-date information about careers and additional assessments of your values, interests, and skills. Most of the systems include accurate details about training and educational opportunities associated with the most popular careers as well as updated descriptions much like those found in the *OOH* and *DOT*.

The Internet and the World Wide Web

Accessing the Internet has become one of the most popular ways to learn about occupational trends and to gather specific information about specific careers. In addition to the list of useful Internet sites that appears at the end of each chapter of this book, you might want to search for topics on your own as well. Any Internet search engine that allows you to search for key topics of interest should work just fine for this purpose.

You might want to keep in mind that many Internet sites can be particularly useful in supporting career exploration and job search strategies for specific populations. For example, many sites offer specific information for particular ethnic groups, students with disabilities, displaced homemakers, and other groups of people with a common bond of some sort.

Informational Interviewing

After you have used print and electronic media to research careers, you'll benefit greatly from interviewing people who are already employed in occupations you're still considering. Informational interviewing may be the most direct and efficient source of career information of all.

Informational interviewing is not job interviewing. When you interview for a job, someone asks you questions. When you interview for information about a career, *you* ask the questions. See the box titled "Informational Interviewing: Questions to Ask About a Potential Career" for a list of questions you may want to ask during an informational interview.

Primary sources for informational interviews are people you already know. Think about whether anyone you know, perhaps one of your friends or family members knows is working in a career you're considering. You can also use your local telephone directory to contact persons who are working in careers you're exploring.

Be aware that some of the people you call may not even have 5 or 10 minutes to speak with you. Don't get

---

Informational Interviewing: Questions to Ask About a Potential Career

- What interested you in this career?
- What preparation did you need for obtaining this job?
- What do you like most about your career?
- What do you like least about your career?
- What are your job responsibilities?
- What kinds of stress do you experience on the job?
- What personal qualities are important in your line of work?
- What are the current prospects and job opportunities in this career?
- Is this career field expanding? In what ways is it changing?
- What is the salary range for persons in this career?
- What are the opportunities for promotion?
- If you were to give advice to someone considering this career, what would it be?
- Are there any sources of information about this career that you're aware of?
- Are there any Web sites you know of that relate to this career?

discouraged. You'll probably be rather surprised at the number of people currently working in a career area who actually get rather excited about the opportunity to talk with someone interested in pursuing the same career that they've selected.

An important first step to this process is setting up the initial appointment. When you introduce yourself to potential interviewees, be sure to explain that you're in the process of exploring different career options. Then tell them that you'd like to spend a few minutes talking with them about their chosen career. You might want to let them know a little bit about your background and why you're considering a career in their field of expertise.

If possible, make an interview appointment at the individual's workplace. This is not only more convenient for the person you interview, but it also gives you an opportunity to witness firsthand the work environment of the career you're considering.

CONSIDER   *Helen*

Helen, a student I worked with a few years ago, discovered the value of informational interviewing as she explored various career options. Helen had been a homemaker for many years. Her youngest child was in fourth grade, and she wanted to return to the workforce. Helen's husband was very supportive of her decision to go back to work and encouraged her to meet with a career counselor to explore the possibilities. She was particularly interested in pursuing a career that directly involved helping others. It also was important for Helen to find a career that offered local employment opportunities. The last thing that she wanted to do was to uproot her family for the sole purpose of locating work.

After meeting with me for a couple of months, Helen narrowed down her list of career options to nursing, teaching, and counseling. The information she gathered from traditional sources, such as the *OOH* and the *Guide to Occupational Exploration,* was somewhat helpful, but she was still having a difficult time figuring out which career would be best for her to pursue. Then we discussed the idea of interviewing current nurses, teachers, and counselors, and Helen agreed that doing so was a good idea.

By talking with current nurses in the area, Helen discovered that there were many openings in nearly every nursing field. Helen was leaning toward psychiatric nursing, one of the specialties for which there was a particular need in her community. Discussions with teachers and counselors in her town revealed the exact opposite situation. Teachers mentioned how difficult it was to find a job in the local market, and counselors described difficulty in finding and maintaining a client base large enough to stay in business. This information was extremely valuable to Helen.

As you might guess, Helen decided to become a registered nurse. When I last spoke with her, she was in her fourth year of employment at one of the hospitals in her community.

As you can see, informational interviews can be very helpful sources in career exploration. Don't forget to utilize this option when seeking information about the careers you're considering.

Career Fairs

Many high schools and colleges, as well as large town newspapers and businesses, sponsor career fairs. These are usually day-long events that give you the opportunity to learn about employment options in your community. Many of the major businesses in a particular community attend career fairs to recruit new employees and to answer questions about future employment opportunities. Career fairs can be especially helpful if you're still considering several careers and want to learn about current hiring trends and practices in a particular region.

State Employment Services

Many states operate an employment service (sometimes referred to as the state unemployment office) that can be of great assistance to you throughout the career exploration process. You may even be fortunate enough to live close to a local office of your state's employment service or in a state that provides computerized access to employment information. Your state or county's employment service can help you in a variety of ways. State employment services often have access to information regarding statewide job trends and projections. They can also be a valuable source of information about local training options. If you're unable to locate a local service center, call your state representative or the state government office in your area to inquire about this service.

Community Leaders

Another way to get information about job trends in your city, county, or region is to contact some of the leaders in your community. Chambers of commerce and other business organizations and clubs can offer helpful information as well as networking opportunities. Getting to know business and community leaders can also prove essential to securing employment. Try to make some of these valuable contacts as you continue the career exploration process.

Friends and Family

Countless clients have reminded me over the years that friends and family members can be sources of helpful information about careers. As you begin narrowing down your career options, don't forget to get feedback from those who know you best.

National Career Development Association

The National Career Development Association (NCDA) is a national organization of career counseling professionals. Each year the NCDA compiles a listing of current career literature that you may find helpful as you explore various career options. The list is published each summer in the association's journal, *The Career Development Quarterly*. Information about the journal and other publications sponsored by the NCDA is available on the NCDA Web site at www.ncda.org.

Local Trade Associations and Unions

Another way to gather accurate information about various occupations is to contact local trade associations and unions. They'll be glad to provide you with information about local job trends, working conditions, and projected employment opportunities. You'll find contact information for trade associations and unions in your yellow pages.

CONSIDER   *Emma*

Emma, a recent client of mine, was interested in a career as a heating and air conditioning repairperson. She obtained some general information about the career on the OOH Internet site (http://stats.bls.gov/ocohome.htm) and by reading several recently published articles in newspapers and magazines available at her local library. But the information that she reported to be most helpful was provided by the local heating, ventilation, and air conditioning (HVAC) union. Union representatives sent Emma a brochure that explained the process of becoming an HVAC apprentice, something that is required to become a member of the local union. After meeting with the president of the local union, Emma obtained an apprenticeship assignment with one of the local workers in town. She recently completed her training and apprenticeship program and is now a member of the local union, earning over $55,000 a year!

Completing Exercise 6.1, "Using the Career Information Form," for each of the careers you're considering at this time will help you summarize the information you gather about those careers from the resources described in this chapter.

EXERCISE 6.1   *USING THE CAREER INFORMATION FORM*

Two blank Career Information Forms appear at the end of the chapter. Feel free to make additional copies so that you can complete this exercise for each of the careers you're exploring.

In the space provided at the top of each form, write in the careers that you'd like to learn more about. You might want to look back at the short list you generated at the end of Chapter 5. Using the various sources of information discussed in this chapter, try to find answers to as many of the questions about each career as possible.

Don't get discouraged if it takes a few days or weeks to complete this project. You may have to consult several different sources before finding out all of the information for each career you're considering. The career decisions you'll be making are going to directly influence many aspects of your life. Devoting a substantial amount of time and energy to this process is well worth the investment!

The sample below will give you an idea of how you might go about completing these forms. The information to complete the sample form was obtained from several sources, including the O*NET Web site, the *OOH*, the *Encyclopedia of Careers and Vocational Guidance*, a few newspaper articles, informational interviews with computer programmers, and DISCOVER (one of the computerized career information and guidance systems mentioned earlier).

A Sample Career Information Form

GENERAL INFORMATION

Title of Career: Computer Programmer

NATURE OF WORK

General Working Conditions: Computer programmers usually work in offices that are relatively comfortable and quiet. Some programmers work long hours or on weekends to meet deadlines. Many programmers are beginning to work out of their homes as they seek opportunities to engage in telecommuting or consulting work.

Employee Responsibilities: Computer programmers write specific programs by breaking down each step into a logical series of instructions the computer can follow. They then code these instructions in a conventional programming language, such as COBOL; an artificial intelligence language, such as Prolog; or a more advanced language, such as Java, C++, or Visual Basic. Many programmers also are involved in updating, repairing, modifying, and expanding existing programs.

Physical Demands: Sometimes long hours of sedentary work are required, often at a desk or in an office setting.

Potential Work Hazards: Computer programmers are susceptible to eyestrain, back discomfort, and hand and wrist problems, such as carpal tunnel syndrome.

EMPLOYMENT TRENDS AND PROJECTIONS

Current Supply and Demand for Workers: About 650,000 computer programmers were working in 1998 in a variety of industries. Most programmers probably work for companies that provide engineering and management services, telecommunications companies, manufacturers of computer equipment, and government agencies.

Future Prospects: Employment of programmers is expected to grow faster than average over the next several years.

Stability of Employment: Because of the need for companies and organizations to keep up with constantly updated technologies, most computer programmers—once hired—are able to remain relatively stable in their work roles.

Opportunities for Advancement: There are many opportunities for computer programmers to advance into managerial or higher-paying programming positions over time. Advanced positions in computer programming may include lead programmer, programming analyst, and research and development manager. Many programmers elect to begin small companies or businesses or opt to serve in a consultation role as a means of employment.

QUALIFICATIONS

General Qualifications for Employment: Required skills vary from job to job, but most programmers are expected to be proficient in a number of computer programming languages, especially the newer, object-oriented programming languages, such as C++, Visual Basic, and Java.

Educational/Training Requirements: Because of the growing number of qualified applicants and the increasing complexity of many programming tasks, bachelor's degrees are commonly required, although some programmers can still find good jobs with a two-year degree or certificate. Still, it's probably the case that most employers will hire someone with lots of experience even if the person lacks a particular degree or formal training credential. Recent college graduates can usually improve their employment prospects by participating in a college work-study program or by completing an internship.

Minimum Aptitude: Again, this varies from company to company, but employers tend to look for candidates who possess the necessary programming skills *and* who can think logically and pay close attention to details. Computer programming jobs tend to require patience, persistence, and the ability to work on exacting analytical work, especially under pressure.

Preparation Standards: Completion of *at least* a two-year certificate or degree program is necessary; a bachelor's degree is probably a better idea. Some internship or cooperative learning experience would probably be a good idea, too. Learning several programming languages will increase employment opportunities. Professional certification also may provide a job seeker in this field a competitive advantage.

WORKLOAD AND SALARY INFORMATION

Typical Hours Worked Each Week/Month: Although most programmers average between 40 and 50 hours of work a week, their hours are sometimes flexible (depending on the particular company they work for). Most programmers are "on salary" and are not hourly employees. As a result, they do not necessarily get compensated for overtime work.

Salary Range: Median annual earnings of computer programmers in 1998 were $47,550, with the middle 50 percent of programmers earning between $36,020 and $70,610. Starting salary offers for graduates with a bachelor's degree in computer programming averaged $40,800 a year in 1999. Average starting salaries for Internet programmers ranged a bit higher in 1999 (from $48,800 to $68,300).

Benefits: Besides the usual health, dental, vision, and retirement benefits that vary from company to company, most computer programmers have the luxury of working on some of the most powerful and advanced computers available.

RELATED OCCUPATIONS

Computer scientist, computer engineer, systems analyst, operations research analyst, database administrator

SOURCES OF ADDITIONAL INFORMATION

Institute for Certification of Computing Professionals (ICCP), 2200 East Devon Avenue, Suite 268, Des Plaines, IL 60018; www.iccp.org.

The Association for Computing Machinery (ACM), 1515 Broadway, New York, NY 10036; www.acm.org.

Institute of Electrical and Electronics Engineers-United States of America, 1828 L. Street NW, Suite 1202, Washington, DC 20036; www.ieee.org.

JOB SHADOWING

In addition to gathering the information to complete the Career Information Forms, another effective method to help you narrow down your career options is **job shadowing.** Job shadowing refers to a hands-on exercise in which you learn about many of the day-to-day tasks and responsibilities associated with careers you're considering. When you job shadow, you actually follow workers around (as if you were their shadow) as they engage in the various duties associated with their jobs.

Job shadowing can teach you about many of the day-to-day tasks and responsibilities associated with the careers you're considering.

The benefits of job shadowing are numerous. Not only will you be able to get a firsthand sense of what employment in particular careers is really all about, but you might also have the opportunity to make some important job contacts that could come in handy in the future.

| Samantha | CONSIDER |

Samantha, a young woman I once worked with, expected to have a very rough time breaking into the male-dominated field of carpentry. She had a strong interest in carpentry as a profession, but was afraid she might be discriminated against because of her gender. During exploration of this career option, I encouraged Samantha to job shadow with a local carpenter in town.

After the job-shadowing experience, Samantha became even more committed to pursuing a career in carpentry. Furthermore, the person whom Samantha "shadowed" ended up offering her summer employment with his company and eventually a full-time position. By taking the time to engage in job shadowing, Samantha not only had the opportunity to see what type of work a carpenter does on a daily basis, but she also reaped the benefit of obtaining an actual job that she might not have even applied for in the first place.

Exercise 6.2, "Job Shadowing," will help you prepare for and evaluate your job shadowing experiences.

| JOB SHADOWING | EXERCISE 6.2 |

A. First, decide which careers you'd like to job shadow. Based on the results of the previous exercise, you may have already started the process of narrowing down your list of preferred careers. Consider job shadowing each career you're still exploring.

List below those careers that you'd like to job shadow:

1. _____
2. _____
3. _____
4. _____
5. _____

B. The next step is to contact individuals who are currently working in the careers you've listed. Many of the resources described in this chapter can provide you with helpful information in this regard. You'll probably have the best results in locating someone to shadow by using the telephone directory, contacting local community leaders, checking with trade organizations and associations, and asking friends and family members for contacts. Local offices of the state employment service and your local college's career center may also be able to help you with this task.

Try to get in touch with the company's human resources director if you don't already know an employee you can observe on the job. The human resources director will probably be able to provide you with general information regarding job shadowing at that company, as well as put you in contact with particular employees you might be able to shadow. Don't assume that the person you talk with will know what "job shadowing" is all about. Explain that you're in the process of making some career decisions and that you'd like to observe the work that goes on in their setting for a few hours.

It might be a good idea to job shadow the same career more than once, with employees from different companies or organizations. You probably won't be making any definitive conclusions about a career based solely on job shadowing. Still, with only one shadowing experience for a particular career option, you risk getting a biased view of that career.

C. You'll have the opportunity during the job-shadowing exercise to observe a variety of things about the nature of a particular career. Pay especially close attention to those details that are likely to influence your decision of whether or not to continue pursuing a career in that particular industry. Take a look at the Job Shadow Evaluation Form before engaging in your first shadowing experience to get an idea of some of the important questions you should be thinking about during the exercise.

D. Make as many copies of the Job Shadow Evaluation Form as you need. After each of your job-shadowing experiences, use the form to evaluate your experience. As you complete the forms, focus on information you learned about the career that you weren't aware of prior to job shadowing.

THE VALUE OF PART-TIME AND VOLUNTEER EXPERIENCES

Perhaps the most comprehensive method for gathering information about potential careers is to obtain actual part-time or volunteer work experience. Working with high school and college students over the years, I've been constantly reminded that one of the best ways to learn about a career is to obtain on-the-job experience. Although it may not always be easy to identify part-time or volunteer work that's available in the career fields you're interested in, you may be surprised by how many opportunities actually exist for you to obtain such experience.

Part-time or volunteer work is a useful method of gathering information about potential careers.

If obtaining part-time work in careers you're considering isn't easy, then you might try getting some experience in a field that's related to your career interests. Someone who's considering a career as a financial planner, for example, may not find any jobs or volunteer experiences in financial planning per se, but there may be other part-time opportunities available related to financial planning. Work as a bank teller or tax assistant might at least let you see what occupations related to financial management are all about.

Working part-time or volunteering in a career you're exploring will allow you to see if it's the right career for you.

CONSIDER *Michael*

Michael, a student I worked with several years ago, is a perfect example of how obtaining valuable part-time work experience can be beneficial during career exploration. Michael was fairly confident that he wanted to be a gerontological counselor (a counselor who works with the elderly). All indications from the career assessments Michael completed seemed to support his decision.

Michael grew up in a poverty-stricken neighborhood in the Southwest and spent a lot of his time as a young man caring for his grandparents and many of the other older citizens in his community. He explained to me that he was rather confident that he wanted a career that would provide him with the opportunity to work with older people on a regular basis.

A few months after we began working together, Michael was fortunate enough to find a volunteer position working at a local nursing home. A couple of weeks later, I asked Michael how working at the nursing home was going, and he responded that he wasn't having much fun at all. He explained that working with the elderly was very different than he thought it would be. Michael still wanted to pursue a career in the helping professions, but he had learned—based *directly* on his volunteer experience—that working with the elder-

Job Shadow Evaluation Form

Title of Career: _____

Job Shadow Date and Time: _____

Business Name: _____

Address: _____

Contact Person: _____ Phone: _____

Job Title: _____

GENERAL WORKING CONDITIONS:

_____

_____

_____

_____

_____

TASKS AND DUTIES:

_____

_____

_____

_____

_____

THINGS I LEARNED ABOUT THAT I DIDN'T ALREADY KNOW:

_____

_____

_____

_____

_____

OVERALL IMPRESSIONS OF THE JOB:

_____

_____

_____

_____

_____

ly was not the best option for him after all. When you consider that preparation for a career as a gerontological counselor includes the completion of a bachelor's degree followed by at least two years of graduate school and a year of internship, you begin to see the value of Michael's volunteer experience.

Many academic departments at colleges and universities have established relationships with companies and organizations within the community that offer part-time work or volunteer opportunities. Career centers on most college campuses offer a variety of internship and cooperative learning activities that may be able to provide you with similar experiences. Connections you may have through a religious or community service organization might also help you identify potential sites for obtaining volunteer work experience associated with your career options. Appendix D provides a brief overview of several job search strategies that you might find helpful as you search for part-time or volunteer job openings.

SURFING THE WEB WITH A PURPOSE

www.state.nj.us/njded/voc/shadowtoc.htm New Jersey's School to Career Office created a very comprehensive handbook on job shadowing. At this site you'll be able to download a copy of the handbook, as long as you have Adobe Acrobat (PDF) capabilities on your computer.

http://danenet.wicip.org/jets/jet-9407-p.html This is one of the best sites on the Internet for learning more about informational interviewing. It's concise yet descriptive, outlining steps to follow to conduct an effective informational interview. It includes 20 specific questions you might want to ask those persons whom you interview as part of the informational interviewing exercise.

www.advancingwomen.com/career/career_interview.html This site, sponsored by Advancing Women Careers, also provides excellent information about informational interviewing, including a list of goals that should be accomplished during an informational interview, a list of 18 potential interview questions, and several helpful links.

www.acinet.org/acinet/ This site could probably be listed at the end of just about any chapter of this book. It is a very useful resource, with more than 100 links to a variety of sites, arranged in six categories: General Outlook, Wages and Trends, Employer Search, State Profile, Resource Library, and Career Exploration.

QUESTIONS FOR CRITICAL THOUGHT

1. Which of the resources described in this chapter do you think will be most useful to you as you gather important information about careers you're considering? Why do you think these particular resources will be most helpful?
2. How can accessing the on-line, interactive version of the OOH (http://stats.bls.gov/ocohome.htm) help you make effective career decisions?
3. What are some of the benefits that come from engaging in job shadowing as a method of career exploration?
4. How might you go about searching for a part-time job or volunteer experience in a career that you're currently considering?

Career Information Form

Title of Career: _____

NATURE OF WORK

General Working Conditions:

_____
_____
_____
_____

Employee Responsibilities:

_____
_____
_____
_____

Physical Demands:

_____
_____
_____
_____

Potential Work Hazards:

_____
_____
_____
_____

EMPLOYMENT TRENDS AND PROJECTIONS

Current Supply and Demand for Workers:

_____

Future Prospects:

_____
_____
_____

Stability of Employment:

_____

_____

_____

_____

Opportunities for Advancement:

_____

_____

_____

_____

QUALIFICATIONS

General Qualifications for Employment:

_____

_____

_____

_____

Educational/Training Requirements:

_____

_____

_____

_____

Minimum Aptitude:

_____

_____

_____

_____

Preparation Standards:

_____

_____

_____

_____

WORKLOAD AND SALARY INFORMATION

Typical Hours Worked Each Week/Month:

_____

_____

_____

Salary Range:

_____

_____

_____

Benefits:

_____

_____

_____

_____

RELATED OCCUPATIONS

_____

_____

_____

_____

_____

_____

SOURCES OF ADDITIONAL INFORMATION

_____

_____

_____

_____

_____

_____

Career Information Form

Title of Career: _____

NATURE OF WORK

General Working Conditions:

_____
_____
_____
_____

Employee Responsibilities:

_____
_____
_____
_____

Physical Demands:

_____
_____
_____
_____

Potential Work Hazards:

_____
_____
_____
_____

EMPLOYMENT TRENDS AND PROJECTIONS

Current Supply and Demand for Workers:

_____

Future Prospects:

_____
_____
_____

Stability of Employment:

_____

_____

_____

_____

Opportunities for Advancement:

_____

_____

_____

_____

QUALIFICATIONS

General Qualifications for Employment:

_____

_____

_____

_____

Educational/Training Requirements:

_____

_____

_____

_____

Minimum Aptitude:

_____

_____

_____

_____

Preparation Standards:

_____

_____

_____

_____

WORKLOAD AND SALARY INFORMATION

Typical Hours Worked Each Week/Month:

_____

_____

_____

Salary Range:

_____

_____

_____

Benefits:

_____

_____

_____

_____

_____

RELATED OCCUPATIONS

_____

_____

_____

_____

_____

_____

_____

SOURCES OF ADDITIONAL INFORMATION

_____

_____

_____

_____

_____

_____

_____

Facing the challenges head-on

IDENTIFYING AND OVERCOMING THE HURDLES

A s you narrow down your career options, it will be increasingly important for you to consider your chances of achieving your various career goals. One of the best ways to engage in that process is to consider potential hurdles that may interfere with your career development and then to develop strategies to overcome them.

The primary purpose of this chapter is to introduce you to the types of hurdles, or barriers, that could interfere with your chances of success in the careers you're exploring. You'll learn about the differences between internal and external barriers as well as real versus perceived barriers. You will read several case studies to gain a clearer understanding of the roles that barriers play in the career decision-making process. You'll also have the opportunity to learn about effective strategies for overcoming those barriers.

THE ROLE OF BARRIERS IN CAREER DECISION MAKING

Career counselors have long recognized the role that barriers play in the career decision-making process. Barriers are those obstacles that may deter you from reaching a particular career goal. Whether the information we have about particular barriers is accurate or not, we often compromise our career goals based on the barriers we perceive. If we *believe* that a certain career is not possible because of certain barriers, then we might compromise our goals and consider alternative career options instead. But recognizing the barriers to achieving our career goals doesn't have to result in compromise. The more we're aware of potential barriers, the more likely we are to be prepared when we actually face them. This process begins with an understanding of the different types of barriers that can occur throughout the career decision-making process.

Many of the barriers that influence our career decisions are referred to as *internal* barriers. These are barriers that come from inside of us. We usually have a fair amount of control over internal barriers and, through hard work and effort, can often overcome them. A lack of confidence in your ability to complete a degree, procrastination, poor study habits, the fear of failure, and concerns about juggling multiple life roles are just a few examples of internal barriers.

Other kinds of career-related barriers are referred to as *external* barriers. These are barriers that come from sources outside of us. We usually have very little, if any, control over these barriers. Global economic trends, educational requirements associated with a particular career, discrim- ination, and employment projections are examples of external barriers. Although we have a more difficult time controlling external barriers, identifying them can help us achieve our career goals.

Internal barriers come from inside of us, whereas external barriers come from sources outside of us.

Some common examples of internal and external barriers are listed in the box titled, "Examples of Internal and External Barriers." Although this listing of barriers is certainly not all-encompassing, it does give you an idea of the differences between internal and external barriers, a distinction that may be helpful to you as you consider the kinds of barriers associated with some of your career possibilities.

Many people consider various aspects of their cultural background to be potential barriers to career development. Sometimes a person will view her racial background, gender, sexual orientation, religious beliefs, socioeconomic status, or physical disability as a barrier to career success. These factors can be perceived as especially problematic if you expect them to lead to discrimination and prejudice on the job. The important thing to remember is that countless resources exist to help you overcome these and other related barriers.

In terms of employment discrimination on the basis of age, gender, racial and ethnic background, religious beliefs, sexual orientation, and disability status, you need to remember that discrimination in *any* form is illegal. Employers are required to hire people on the basis of their qualifications, not their age, gender, race, religion, sexual orientation, or disability status. Still, you may find it useful to contact labor organizations in your area that can offer support in your efforts to secure a career in a particular field. If you have any doubt regarding your treatment in an employment setting, contact the Equal Employment Opportunity/Affirmative Action office in your community.

Examples of Internal and External Barriers

INTERNAL BARRIERS

- Anxiety associated with making career decisions
- Concerns about multiple life roles and responsibilities
- Fear of failure
- Low confidence in your ability to obtain a particular degree
- Poor study habits
- Procrastination

EXTERNAL BARRIERS

- Economic trends
- Educational requirements
- Employment outlook
- Job discrimination
- Lack of local educational/training opportunities
- Lack of funds available to pursue a career

Persons with disabilities, both physical and mental in nature, often wonder how they'll be able to engage in certain kinds of work given their particular disability. Knowledge about available resources is a key factor to overcoming these potential barriers. The Americans with Disabilities Act (ADA), passed in 1990, protects all individuals from job discrimination on the basis of disabilities (which covers all physiological conditions affecting one or more of the body's systems as well as mental and psychological disorders). Visual, hearing, and speech impairments, cerebral palsy, epilepsy, muscular dystrophy, multiple sclerosis, HIV, cancer, diabetes, emotional illness, and learning disabilities are just a few of the types of disabilities protected under the law.

In her book *Job Strategies for People with Disabilities*, Melanie Witt explains that prospective employers must provide "reasonable accommodations" to employees who have a disability of some sort. These accommodations can range from making a building more accessible to offering variable work hours to employees with special needs. Special equipment might be purchased or changes in the work environment might be made to help employees complete their tasks more efficiently.

Most college and universities have someone who is responsible for assisting students with disabilities in all aspects of their educational and career development. The Dean of Students office would be able to direct you to the appropriate resources on your campus. To find out more about the services available to persons with disabilities in your state, contact the state government office responsible for ensuring compliance with ADA regulations. You might also want to contact the Department of Justice, Office for ADA Information, P.O. Box 66118, Washington, DC 20035. The ADA Hotline is (202) 514-0301, and the Web site address is www.usdoj.gov/crt/ada.

REAL AND PERCEIVED BARRIERS

As you begin to think about the kinds of barriers that are relevant to your life situation, you'll also want to distinguish between *real* and *perceived* barriers.

Gloria	CONSIDER

Gloria, a student I once worked with, had decided that she was going to go back to school to pursue a degree in criminal justice. Gloria was in her late forties, and her two children were grown and living on their own. Gloria had always thought about returning to school to become qualified to work in law enforcement. With more free time on her hands, Gloria decided to begin to make that dream a reality.

Like many people who return to the world of work after several years away, Gloria was starting to wonder if she really had what it takes to succeed in an academic training program. She had made a list of obstacles that she believed were likely to interfere with her career goal. As I reviewed her list of barriers, I was curious about how accurate Gloria's perceptions were of the hurdles she had put on her list.

One of the barriers Gloria had listed, for example, was weak writing skills. When I asked her how she had reached that conclusion, she mentioned that it had been almost 25 years since she had written a formal paper in school. When I asked if she had received any recent feedback about her writing skills, she began to realize that her perception wasn't based on actual feedback, but rather on her hunch that she *probably* had poor written communication skills relative to other college students.

As Gloria and I continued working together, it became increasingly apparent to both of us that many of the barriers she had listed were not really as problematic as she had originally thought. Her results on the college placement tests, for example, revealed that Gloria's writing skills were actually above average for college students. The increased awareness that came from our discussion of barriers and the results of actual skills assessments proved to be very useful in helping Gloria make more informed career decisions.

Sometimes determining whether barriers are real or perceived is a difficult thing to do.

Several years ago I worked with Monique, a 42-year-old Native American woman who was recovering from a stroke. When Monique and I first met, she had narrowed down her career options to legal secretary, medical office receptionist, and preschool teacher. After Monique gathered ample information about these various options, I asked her to think about the types of barriers associated with each potential career.

Barriers related to a career as a preschool teacher that Monique identified included (1) her difficulty in engaging in strenuous physical activities and (2) the educational requirements associated with becoming a teacher. Barriers associated with work as a legal secretary and medical receptionist included (1) the physical pain she experienced when sitting for long periods of time and (2) the problems she had been experiencing with her eyesight. Monique was concerned that she might have some difficulty reading transcripts and other legal documents. Monique was also concerned about her financial situation and its impact on all of her career options.

Monique also identified many social hindrances that could potentially serve as barriers to her career goals. Her parents were both getting rather old and were in need of daily care. Her husband and children were encouraging her to stay home and spend more time recovering from her stroke. Friends were offering their suggestions as to what she should do. Everyone seemed to have an opinion about what was best for Monique. She was clearly aware that her career decision was going to have an impact on the lives of others.

Paying close attention to the potential barriers associated with each career on her short list, Monique decided to pursue part-time work as a medical office receptionist, something she had a couple of years experience with prior to her stroke. Taking the time to think about the many different barriers that could influence her satisfaction and success proved to be very helpful to Monique.

In Chapter 8 you'll be narrowing down your list of career options even further than you have already. But before you make those decisions, think about the potential barriers that might develop as you continue to engage in the career exploration process. After developing a list of potential career-related barriers, you'll be able to work on identifying very specific methods for overcoming those barriers.

Think about the potential barriers that might develop as you continue the career exploration process.

Identifying barriers is much simpler for some people than it is for others. Many people are already aware of the barriers that stand in their way of reaching the goals they've set for themselves. Others need some help identifying them. Furthermore, many barriers—both internal and external—can seem like insurmountable obstacles. But identifying specific barriers associated with careers can help you determine what steps you need to take in order to overcome those hurdles.

A few years ago I worked with Juan, a high school senior who was very interested in becoming a professional athlete. His parents were concerned that by focusing on a career in professional sports, Juan was "ignoring other careers" that he might be more likely to succeed in. Juan was a first-generation college student. In fact, he was the only one in his family ever to graduate from high school. His parents, both of whom came from a low socioeconomic background, wanted to do all that they possibly could to ensure Juan's success.

I asked Juan to outline his career goals. As expected, he explained that he was really only interested in pursuing a career as a professional athlete. When I asked Juan to explain reasons for his interest in professional sports, it became apparent that he enjoyed the outdoors, found satisfaction in a competitive environment, and liked the possibility of earning (as he put it) "a whole lot of money."

I then asked Juan to outline some of the potential barriers that might interfere with his career goal. His initial response was that there really weren't any barriers, no reason at all to think that he wouldn't succeed in professional sports. The way he looked at it, because he had already received numerous awards in high school in athletics, he had no reason to think that succeeding in professional sports would be any different. My purpose in working with Juan wasn't to persuade him to change his mind about a career in professional sports, nor did I want to decrease Juan's confidence in his abilities. I simply wanted him to recognize that there might be some potential barriers to becoming a professional athlete—just as there are for any career option.

To assist Juan in the process of considering potential barriers, I encouraged him to talk with some of his friends and family members. I also arranged for Juan to interview three professional athletes I knew and talk with them about some of the barriers that they had experienced over the years. After Juan followed my suggestion, I asked him to develop a list of potential barriers based on what he had learned. As I had hoped, Juan was eventually able to cite several barriers, both external and internal, that he hadn't considered before.

Juan still decided to pursue a career as a professional athlete. And, as of the publication of this book, Juan is actually playing professional baseball! After considering all of the potential barriers to becoming a professional athlete and establishing ways to overcome them, Juan was able to proceed with his career goal with increased knowledge and confidence.

The experiences of Gloria, Monique, and Juan illustrate why identifying potential barriers to career goals is so important. By evaluating perceived barriers, Gloria was able to obtain a more realistic appraisal of her skills. By considering the various internal and external barriers associated with her career options, Monique was able to make an accurate assessment of the best career option for her to pursue. And by identifying possible barriers related to becoming a professional athlete, Juan was better able to prepare to meet the challenges that he encountered along the way.

Exercise 7.1 is designed to help you generate a list of potential barriers associated with the career options you're still exploring. It's important to consider all barriers, internal *and* external, associated with each of your career options. Exercises 7.2 and 7.3 will help you develop strategies for overcoming those barriers as you begin clearing the way for the final stages of the career exploration and planning process.

IDENTIFYING CAREER-RELATED BARRIERS   EXERCISE 7.1

We're best able to identify potential barriers to a particular career goal when we draw on many different sources of information. Of course, you're the best person to determine which barriers are most applicable to your particular life situation. But talking with friends, family members, and other persons in your life may help you identify a few barriers that you might not otherwise come up with on your own.

All of the information that you've gathered up to this point about the world of work will probably help you identify many of the internal and external barriers associated with careers you're considering. Consult that information and talk with the people who know you best as you work on developing your lists of barriers for each career option.

CAREER OPTION: _____

INTERNAL BARRIERS:

_____

_____

_____

_____

EXTERNAL BARRIERS:

_____

_____

_____

_____

CAREER OPTION: _____

INTERNAL BARRIERS:

_____

_____

_____

_____

EXTERNAL BARRIERS:

_____

_____

_____

_____

CAREER OPTION: _____

INTERNAL BARRIERS:

_____

_____

_____

_____

EXTERNAL BARRIERS:

_____

_____

_____

_____

CAREER OPTION: _____

INTERNAL BARRIERS:

_____
_____
_____
_____

EXTERNAL BARRIERS:

_____
_____
_____
_____

CAREER OPTION: _____

INTERNAL BARRIERS:

_____
_____
_____
_____

EXTERNAL BARRIERS:

_____
_____
_____
_____

CAREER OPTION: _____

INTERNAL BARRIERS:

_____
_____
_____
_____

EXTERNAL BARRIERS:

_____
_____
_____
_____

You'll refer to these lists of barriers later in the chapter as you begin to develop strategies for overcoming them.

CAREER SELF-EFFICACY AND ITS RELATIONSHIP TO BARRIERS

The contributions of Dr. Albert Bandura, one of the world's most renowned psychologists, have helped us gain important insights into human behavior. One of Dr. Bandura's contributions that has been especially helpful in the area of career counseling is the concept of self-efficacy.

Self-efficacy is an individual's confidence in his or her ability to accomplish a specific task.

Self-efficacy is an individual's confidence in his or her ability to accomplish a specific task. For example, if a 300-pound barbell were sitting on the floor in front of me, and you asked me how confident I was in my ability to dead-lift the barbell on a scale of one (no confidence at all) to five (very high confidence), I would respond by saying "one." My confidence level is very low when it comes to lifting large amounts of weight. Dr. Bandura would say that I have low self-efficacy for lifting the 300-pound barbell. My particular level of self-efficacy for lifting a 300-pound barbell is influenced by several different factors, which we will discuss shortly.

This concept of self-efficacy directly applies to overcoming career-related barriers. For instance, if you're not very confident in your ability to overcome certain barriers, then it would be appropriate to say that you have low self-efficacy for overcoming those barriers. If, on the other hand, you believe that you can overcome many potential career barriers without much of a problem, then it would be appropriate to say you have high self-efficacy for overcoming those barriers.

One of the most interesting things that Dr. Bandura and other researchers have found about self-efficacy is that the likelihood of successfully completing a particular task is directly linked with your level of self-efficacy associated with that task. To put it another way, if you're confident in your ability to accomplish something, then odds are that you'll be successful at accomplishing it. If, on the other hand, you aren't very confident in your ability to complete a task, then odds are that you'll fail at it.

Identifying barriers for certain career options is only the beginning of the process. Once you've identified particular barriers related to the careers you're exploring, you need to work on increasing your confidence (or self-efficacy) and your skills for overcoming those barriers. Granted, there may be many barriers (especially external barriers) that simply cannot be overcome. There isn't a whole lot you can do, for example, to overcome problems with the global economy. But there may be lots you can do to overcome many of the barriers you listed in Exercise 7.1.

If you're confident in your ability to accomplish something, odds are that you will accomplish it.

CONSIDER *Anna*

Consider the case of Anna. Anna was an 18-year-old, first-year community college student. She had been diagnosed with multiple sclerosis at the end of her senior year of high school. School work had always been a challenge for Anna, and academic work in college was no exception. Her physical condition was becoming especially challenging, and Anna was beginning to think that because of her disability, obtaining a college degree might not be possible after all.

Instead of giving up, however, Anna decided to contact the Dean of Students to find out if there were any services on campus that she could access. She discovered that there was an Office of Special Student Services that could assist with her educational and career concerns. After meeting with the Director of Special Student Services, Anna realized that *many* support services were available to empower her to succeed. Her confidence or self-efficacy for obtaining a college degree increased dramatically because she took the time to explore sources of support available right on campus.

Increasing your confidence in your ability to accomplish your career goals can play an important role in career decision making. This is especially true when it comes to your confidence or self-efficacy for overcoming career-related barriers. Let's take a closer look at Dr. Bandura's concept of self-efficacy.

Dr. Bandura explained that four factors contribute to our level of self-efficacy for a particular task.

- *Previous Experiences* (or Performance Accomplishments)
  Past experiences we've had performing the task.

- *Vicarious Learning*
  Learning about our own abilities to accomplish a task by watching others.

- *Verbal Persuasion*
  The degree to which other people around us persuade or encourage us to accomplish a task.

- *Physiological Arousal*
  How excited or anxious we get as we try to accomplish a task.

To get a better idea of how these factors influence our self-efficacy, let's return to the 300-pound barbell example. In terms of *previous experiences*, I know that I have *never* been able to dead-lift any more than 220 pounds (and only that much on a *very* good day). Because of these past experiences, I'm fairly sure that I lack the ability to lift a 300-pound barbell. If I had been able to lift 300 pounds in the past, or at least some amount of weight closer to it (say 275 or 280 pounds), then my self-efficacy for lifting 300 pounds would be much higher.

Increasing your self-efficacy for overcoming career-related barriers can play an important role in career decision making.

In terms of *vicarious learning*, the second source of self-efficacy, I've learned from watching many of my friends lift weights that none of our bodies are built like the folks who we know are able to lift 300 pounds. In other words, I've learned vicariously (from watching other people) that I'm not likely to successfully lift 300 pounds.

In terms of *verbal persuasion*, I don't recall anyone ever trying to *encourage* me to lift 300 pounds. It's no surprise, then, that my self-efficacy for lifting 300 pounds is so low. Verbal persuasion influences our self-efficacy for accomplishing a task by either encouraging or discouraging us from trying to accomplish it.

The fourth factor that influences our self-efficacy is *physiological arousal.* Psychologists discovered long ago that we tend to perform best when we experience only a moderate degree of anxiety or arousal associated with performing a task. Of course, too much anxiety or arousal can be even more detrimental than no anxiety at all. The lesson here is that a little arousal is not a bad thing. What Dr. Bandura and his colleagues have discovered, as you might expect, is that our self-

efficacy for accomplishing a given task is related to the amount of anxiety we experience when engaging in that task.

There's quite a lot we can do to influence the sources of self-efficacy for any specific task. For instance, consider the role that previous experience plays in the development of our self-efficacy. If we have low self-efficacy for overcoming a particular barrier, then we might need to seek new experiences that will allow us the opportunity to try out different ways to overcome that barrier.

Take, for example, my low self-efficacy for lifting a 300-pound barbell. One way that I might be able to increase my self-efficacy for lifting it would be to identify new experiences that might increase my chances of successfully lifting it in the future. If I were to set up some short-term goals, perhaps increasing my weight-lifting ability to dead-lift 240 pounds by the end of this month, 250 pounds by the end of next month, and perhaps 260 pounds the month after that, I just might increase my chances for eventually lifting 300 pounds.

This process can work for overcoming career-related barriers, too.

CONSIDER *Derrick*

I once worked with a student named Derrick, who had identified poor study habits as a career barrier related to his desire to become a pediatrician. Derrick lived in the inner city in a large metropolitan area in the West. He grew up in an impoverished neighborhood and attributed his poor study skills to financial hardship experienced during his early years. He was beginning to think that his past experiences might keep him from realizing his goal of becoming a pediatrician.

After developing a list of new experiences that might help him overcome this barrier, however, Derrick realized that not knowing how to study properly was probably not such a fatal disaster after all. His list of new experiences included setting up an appointment with the study skills advisor at his college to develop a routine study schedule. This provided Derrick with the opportunity to work on his poor study skills through new *performance accomplishments*.

Just as identifying new experiences can help you overcome specific barriers, so can learning from others who have successfully overcome similar types of barriers (what Dr. Bandura calls *vicarious learning*). I remember suggesting to Derrick that he meet with some of the senior pre-med students at his college to get their advice on how best to establish effective study skills strategies. He engaged in the process of *vicarious learning* by watching others who had successfully overcome the same barrier in the past.

Even the amount of *verbal persuasion* you receive related to overcoming a particular barrier can change over time. One of the best ways to use *verbal persuasion* to your advantage is by interacting with friends who will support and encourage you to overcome the barriers you've identified. Derrick had a lot of friends, two brothers, a sister, and a proud mother, all of whom were helpful in encouraging and supporting his efforts to improve his study habits.

In terms of the influence of *physiological arousal* in career decision making, it's very difficult to make personally rewarding career decisions if you're unable to overcome high levels of anxiety associated with the process. If you experience a considerably high level of anxiety when engaging in career decision-making tasks, then it would probably be a good idea for you to meet with a counselor. Most professional counselors are trained in anxiety reduction strategies and can be a great help to you. Derrick read some self-help books on stress management that his counselor suggested in order to alleviate some of the anxiety he was experiencing related to study skills. It seemed to really help him relax when he was taking notes and studying for tests.

With new performance experiences, exposure to vicarious learning situations, enhanced verbal encouragement, and decreased anxiety, Derrick was well on the way to overcoming his study skills barrier.

You may find that you're fairly confident in your ability to overcome most of the barriers you listed in Exercise 7.1. If so, then you're already well on your way to benefiting from the process of identifying career-related barriers. However, if your self-efficacy for overcoming some of those barriers is less than perfect, Exercise 7.2 may be especially helpful to you.

SELF-EFFICACY CHANGE STRATEGIES	**EXERCISE 7.2**

Part I.

Go back to Exercise 7.1 and rate your self-efficacy for overcoming the barriers that you listed for each career option. Rate your confidence, or self-efficacy level, for each identified barrier on a scale of 1 *(no confidence at all)* to 5 *(complete confidence)*. Write that number in the left margin next to each barrier that you listed. The rating scale shown below can serve as a guide.

1	2	3	4	5
no confidence	*very little confidence*	*some confidence*	*a lot of confidence*	*complete confidence*

Part II.

If your self-efficacy for overcoming a particular barrier is high (4 or 5), then you've probably already identified ways you might overcome that barrier. But if your confidence rating is low, you might want to identify some ways to increase your self-efficacy for overcoming that barrier, if at all possible.

Step 1. Take a look again at the lists of barriers you provided in Exercise 7.1 and select three barriers for which your self-efficacy rating is 2 or lower. Write these barriers in the spaces provided on the Overcoming Identified Barriers section that follows.

Step 2. Think about each barrier you've listed and identify *new experiences* that you might seek in order to help you overcome the barrier. This would be similar to Derrick's decision to meet with the college's study skills advisor and to set up a routine study schedule.

Step 3. List ways that you can use *vicarious learning* and *verbal persuasion* to increase your self-efficacy for overcoming each barrier. Remember that vicarious learning involves discovering ways to overcome barriers by watching and learning from others. Derrick accomplished this by learning from the successful experiences of more experienced pre-med students at the college. Verbal persuasion techniques that may help you overcome specific barriers might include asking your friends and family members to support you in your efforts (as Derrick did) or seeking the assistance of a counselor or academic advisor for ongoing support.

Step 4. Finally, think about strategies you might use to decrease the anxiety associated with each barrier. Recall that Derrick read several self-help books that his counselor recommended. Other strategies you might consider include stress reduction techniques, relaxation exercises, or some other method you've discovered in the past for effectively decreasing anxiety.

Overcoming Identified Barriers

POTENTIAL BARRIER: _____

WAYS TO INCREASE YOUR SELF-EFFICACY FOR OVERCOMING THE BARRIER:

New Experiences

_____

_____

_____

Vicarious Learning

_____

_____

_____

Verbal Persuasion

_____

_____

_____

Anxiety Reduction

_____

_____

_____

POTENTIAL BARRIER: _____

WAYS TO INCREASE YOUR SELF-EFFICACY FOR OVERCOMING THE BARRIER:

New Experiences

_____

_____

_____

Vicarious Learning

_____

_____

_____

Verbal Persuasion

_____

_____

_____

Anxiety Reduction

_____

_____

_____

POTENTIAL BARRIER: _____

WAYS TO INCREASE YOUR SELF-EFFICACY FOR OVERCOMING THE BARRIER:

New Experiences

_____

_____

_____

Vicarious Learning

_____

_____

_____

Verbal Persuasion

_____

_____

_____

Anxiety Reduction

_____

_____

_____

Whether or not you'll be successful in overcoming career-related barriers ultimately depends on how much time and energy you're willing to devote to increasing your self-efficacy for overcoming them. We'll spend some additional time in Chapter 9 identifying other action strategies that will be useful to you in the pursuit of your career goals.

IDENTIFYING HELPFUL RESOURCES

As previously mentioned, friends and family members can be important sources of encouragement and support, not only as you work on identifying and overcoming career-related barriers but throughout the career decision-making process. The social network that your friends and family members provide is often one of the most important—yet often overlooked—sources of support that can help you in your quest to achieve your career goals. In addition to family members and friends, you probably have access to several other individuals who can help you throughout the career decision-making process. These persons might include a career counselor at a college or university, an academic advisor, a favorite teacher, or a recent college graduate.

For each of us, there will be a different list of individuals who can help us throughout the process of making career decisions. Think about the individuals in your life who can serve as your social support network.

The social network provided by your friends and family members is one of the most important sources of support in achieving your career goals.

It's also important to consider other resources available to you during these latter stages of career decision making. You've probably realized by now that many resources are available to help you make effective career decisions. In Chapter 6, we reviewed more than 20 sources of occupational information. In Chapters 3 and 4, you learned about the many types of assessments you can complete to help you learn about your personality, interests, skills, abilities, and values. Many other resources are probably available to you as well. Exercise 7.3 will help you put together a handy list of all resources, including your social support network, that can aid you during the remaining stages of the career exploration and planning process.

EXERCISE 7.3   *RECOGNIZING RESOURCES*

A. Social Support Network

List below the individuals, including friends, family members, and anyone else you are aware of (such as a teacher, advisor, career counselor, or religious leader) who you believe will be helpful as you continue the career decision-making process. Below each person's name and telephone number/E-mail address, list the specific ways that person will be able to help you in the process.

NAME: _____

PHONE NUMBER/E-MAIL: _____

WAYS THIS PERSON CAN HELP ME:

_____

_____

_____

NAME: _____

PHONE NUMBER/E-MAIL: _____

WAYS THIS PERSON CAN HELP ME:

_____

_____

_____

NAME: _____

PHONE NUMBER/E-MAIL: _____

WAYS THIS PERSON CAN HELP ME:

_____

_____

_____

NAME: _____

PHONE NUMBER/E-MAIL: _____

WAYS THIS PERSON CAN HELP ME:

_____

_____

_____

NAME: _____

PHONE NUMBER/E-MAIL: _____

WAYS THIS PERSON CAN HELP ME:

_____

_____

_____

NAME: _____

PHONE NUMBER/E-MAIL: _____

WAYS THIS PERSON CAN HELP ME:

_____

_____

_____

NAME: _____

PHONE NUMBER/E-MAIL: _____

WAYS THIS PERSON CAN HELP ME:

_____

_____

_____

NAME: _____

PHONE NUMBER/E-MAIL: _____

WAYS THIS PERSON CAN HELP ME:

_____

_____

_____

B. Additional Resources

List below all other resources (such as a university career center or local public library) that are available to you as you complete the career decision-making process. Again, be sure to list the specific ways that each resource can help.

RESOURCE: _____

LOCATION: _____

SPECIFIC WAYS THAT THIS RESOURCE WILL BE HELPFUL:

_____

_____

_____

RESOURCE: _____

LOCATION: _____

SPECIFIC WAYS THAT THIS RESOURCE WILL BE HELPFUL:

_____

_____

_____

RESOURCE: _____

LOCATION: _____

SPECIFIC WAYS THAT THIS RESOURCE WILL BE HELPFUL:

_____

_____

_____

RESOURCE: _____

LOCATION: _____

SPECIFIC WAYS THAT THIS RESOURCE WILL BE HELPFUL:

_____

_____

_____

RESOURCE: _____

LOCATION: _____

SPECIFIC WAYS THAT THIS RESOURCE WILL BE HELPFUL:

_____

_____

_____

RESOURCE: _____

LOCATION: _____

SPECIFIC WAYS THAT THIS RESOURCE WILL BE HELPFUL:

_____

_____

_____

RESOURCE: _____

LOCATION: _____

SPECIFIC WAYS THAT THIS RESOURCE WILL BE HELPFUL:

_____

_____

_____

RESOURCE: _____

LOCATION: _____

SPECIFIC WAYS THAT THIS RESOURCE WILL BE HELPFUL:

_____

_____

_____

RESOURCE: _____

LOCATION: _____

SPECIFIC WAYS THAT THIS RESOURCE WILL BE HELPFUL:

_____

_____

_____

RESOURCE: _____

LOCATION: _____

SPECIFIC WAYS THAT THIS RESOURCE WILL BE HELPFUL:

_____

_____

_____

SURFING THE WEB WITH A PURPOSE

http://mentalhelp.net/psyhelp/chap14/chap14u.htm The mentalhelp.net site includes several chapters and articles that deal with a host of psychological topics. This article, "Developing Attitudes that Help You Cope," includes a thorough analysis of Bandura's concept of self-efficacy. As you might imagine, the information found at this site encourages persons to develop high levels of self-efficacy for important tasks, such as career decision making.

http://mentalhelp.net/psyhelp/chap5/chap5g.htm Also part of the mentalhelp.net site, this essay focuses on ways you can reduce anxiety by thinking about perceptions and irrational reactions to those perceptions. Again, Bandura's notion of self-efficacy is discussed—specifically as it relates to physiological arousal and anxiety.

http://eric-web.tc.columbia.edu/digests/dig125.html This article by Jeanne Weiler comes from the Educational Resources in Circulation (ERIC) Clearinghouse on Urban Education. As noted in the title, "Career Development for African American and Latina Females," the article discusses the career development process as experienced by many African American and Latina women. The article is especially relevant to the discussion of perceived barriers presented in this chapter.

www.ed.gov/prog_info/SFA/StudentGuide/ Because limited financial resources often emerges as a significant barrier in the lives of many college students, you might want to review the U. S. Department of Education's site on financial aid. The site includes a link to the federal government's "Student Guide" as well as a link to the Internet version of the Free Application for Federal Student Aid (FAFSA).

QUESTIONS FOR CRITICAL THOUGHT

1. Why is it important for you to identify career-related barriers that you may encounter in the future?
2. Why might an individual develop low self-efficacy for overcoming a particular career-related barrier?
3. How can you increase your self-efficacy for overcoming career-related barriers?
4. Why is it important to identify sources of social support that are available to you during the career decision-making process?

Decisions, decisions, decisions

MAKING A TENTATIVE CAREER DECISION

In Chapter 2, you learned about the five major stages of career development as conceptualized by Dr. Donald Super. You may recall that the growth stage of career development involves learning about ourselves and the world of work in general. Following the growth stage, the exploration stage of development includes the tasks of crystallizing, specifying, and implementing a career choice.

In Chapters 3 and 4, you completed a series of exercises as part of the exploration stage of career development. You completed assessments of your interests, skills, and experiences and evaluated your work and life values. You learned how to combine this information to make more informed career decisions in Chapter 5, and in Chapter 6 you learned about the variety of resources available to you for locating important information about career options.

In Chapter 7 we examined how barriers in the environment and within yourself can sometimes act as stumbling blocks *unless* you develop strategies for overcoming them. With each of these tools, you're prepared to make some tentative decisions about your career.

TENTATIVE CAREER DECISION MAKING

Dr. Super used the term *tentative* when referring to the types of decisions made during career exploration, probably because he recognized that after weeks, months, or even years of exploration, we still might change our minds about the career paths we want to follow. After all, this is an extremely important decision.

That's where Dr. Super's concept of recycling comes in. As we'll discuss in more detail in Chapter 10, the career decisions you're making now will not necessarily be the same career decisions you'll make 10, 15, or 20 years from now. We no longer live in a world where career decisions are made at only one point in our lives. In fact, you'll probably make a career change between five and seven times during your adult life. We're always changing and growing. Our interests, our skills and abilities, our experiences, and even our values change over time. As these

aspects of our self-concept change, so do our ideas about which types of careers are most suitable for us.

Over the next several months (and perhaps even the next year or two) you might want to continue exploring career options. A few weeks of focusing on career decision making is not usually sufficient to make thoughtful career decisions. To the contrary, career exploration is a lifelong process.

Career decisions are no longer made at only one point in our lives.

Nevertheless, in this chapter you'll be asked to select one of the career options you identified back in Chapter 5 as your *tentative* career choice. We'll look at the steps involved in making effective career decisions so that as you recycle through the career decision-making process in the future you'll understand the concepts involved and will be better prepared to make career decisions that count.

CONSIDER   *Cary*

I remember one individual who came to my office rather frustrated about his career development. Cary was about to turn 50 years old, and I was the third career counselor he had seen since he graduated from high school. He couldn't understand why he hadn't selected the right career yet and expressed embarrassment for not knowing, at age 50, what he wanted to do when he "grew up."

Actually, Cary had been very successful in a couple of different careers. After graduating from college at age 23, he started out in the real-estate business working with his parents. His bachelor's degree in marketing and finance came in handy in that career.

After working as a real-estate agent for about 12 years, though, Cary found that the job no longer challenged him the way it once had. After re-evaluating his career interests and abilities and considering his values, Cary decided to pursue a career as a financial planner. For the next five or six years, Cary experienced all of the things that he had been looking for in a career change. He was challenged in ways that he never had been before. He was working with clients who were interested in what he had to say, and he was enjoying greater financial wealth and the flexibility he had hoped for. But after a few years passed, Cary found himself wanting a change yet again.

I posed two key questions to Cary:

- What's wrong with changing careers?
- What's wrong with accepting the fact that your ideal career might actually change over time?

When I asked Cary these questions, he started to realize that his interests, skills, and values had indeed changed over time. He began to think about how these changes had influenced his career development.

Consider some similar questions:

- What's wrong with changing your interests?
- What's wrong with developing new abilities and skills that allow you more flexibility in potential job opportunities?
- What's wrong with realizing that your values can and often do change over time?

Changes in one's occupational status and career direction take a great deal of planning and almost always create some degree of anxiety and stress. That's why career decisions should be thoroughly evaluated before final decisions are made. But there's certainly nothing wrong with exploring new opportunities and allowing yourself the flexibility to make a career change when the time is right.

Think for a moment about all that you've accomplished up to this point in the career decision-making process. A summary of some of the major tasks you've accomplished appears in the box titled "Summary of Career Decision-Making Tasks You've Already Accomplished."

When the process is summarized, you can see how much time and energy you've already devoted to making career decisions. Each of those steps is necessary if you want to make the most effective career decisions that you possibly can. Your task now is to pull together all of the information you've been gathering and make a tentative career decision. Reconsider your values and think about how they influence your career satisfaction and success. You'll want to find a way to maximize the match between your values and the career options you've been considering.

Summary of Career Decision-Making Tasks You've Already Accomplished

1. You've discovered that one of the first things you need to do in order to prepare for making career decisions is to increase your understanding of the world of work, including job trends, occupational projections, and the influence of the economy on employment opportunities.

2. You've learned ways to classify occupations, focusing on Dr. Roe's method of organizing work environments into eight distinct categories: Service, Business Contact, Organization, Technology, Outdoors, Science, General Culture, and Arts and Entertainment.

3. You've learned methods for organizing information that you collect about the world of work in general and about specific careers you're considering.

4. You've recognized the value of mapping out your future and setting goals.

5. You've learned the process of lifelong career development as conceptualized by Dr. Donald Super.

6. You've seen how to determine which stage of the career decision-making process you're in and which tasks are especially helpful as you engage in the career decision-making process.

7. You've completed assessments of your personality, interests, skills, experiences, and values to better understand your career self-concept.

8. You've discovered how to integrate your self-concept as completely as possible when making career decisions.

9. You've learned about a variety of valuable resources you can consult for information about potential career options.

10. You've learned about the roles that perceived barriers play in career decision making, and you've developed strategies for overcoming those barriers.

11. You've identified sources of support that can assist you throughout the career decision-making process, including your social support network and other helpful resources available to you.

PREPARING TO MAKE THE DECISION

The first step to making a tentative career decision is to gather all of the data about the world of work that you've collected and organized. You'll also want to access the information that you've been collecting about each of the career options you've been considering. Take another look at the results of the inventories you completed in Chapters 3 and 4. Even though the results of those assessments were already used to help you make some initial career decisions in Chapter 5, it's a good idea to review them again at this stage of the process.

Find a large table or desk to use. You're going to need plenty of work space as you complete the Career Analysis System described in Exercise 8.1. The more comfortable the setting, the more effective your work during this stage of the process is going to be.

EXERCISE 8.1   *CAREER ANALYSIS SYSTEM*

Step 1. A Career Analysis Form is provided at the end of this chapter. You'll be asked to make several copies of the form *after you complete Steps 1 and 2* so that you can analyze the various career options you've been considering. The example below illustrates the procedure for this exercise. The form looks like this:

SPECIFIC CAREER OPTION: _____			
Values	Value points	Career score	Weighted value
_____	_____	_____	_____
_____	_____	_____	_____
_____	_____	_____	_____
_____	_____	_____	_____
_____	_____	_____	_____
_____	_____	_____	_____
_____	_____	_____	_____
_____	_____	_____	_____
_____	_____	_____	_____
		CAREER POINT TOTAL:	_____

First list the values, both work-related and other core life values, that you identified in Chapter 4 and ranked in order of importance.

Copy both the work-related and core life values lists from Chapter 4 into the first column of your Career Analysis Form under the heading "Values," as shown in the example below:

SPECIFIC CAREER OPTION: _____			
Values	Value points	Career score	Weighted value
Time with family	_____	_____	_____
Flexible work schedule	_____	_____	_____
Stable income	_____	_____	_____
Opportunity for creativity	_____	_____	_____
Opportunity for promotion	_____	_____	_____
Social interaction	_____	_____	_____
Opportunity to write	_____	_____	_____
Health insurance	_____	_____	_____
Professional atmosphere	_____	_____	_____
		CAREER POINT TOTAL:	_____

Step 2. Now think about the values that you listed in the first column of your Career Analysis Form and assign numerical points to each of them. The points that you assign will represent the importance of each value to your career goals. Use the following guidelines for assigning numerical points to each value.

- The points you assign to all of the values on your form should total 100 points (no more and no less).

- These points represent the relative importance that *you* give to each of the values.

- Do not assign two or more values the same number of value points *unless* you want them to be equally weighted in your career decision.

- The more points you assign a given factor, the more that factor will become a part of your career decision.

SPECIFIC CAREER OPTION: _____			
Values	Value points	Career score	Weighted value
Time with family	30		
Flexible work schedule	15		
Stable income	10		
Opportunity for creativity	10		
Opportunity for promotion	7		
Social interaction	7		
Opportunity to write	7		
Health insurance	7		
Professional atmosphere	7		
	CAREER POINT TOTAL: _____		

(The value point column should add up to exactly 100 points.)

Step 3. *Now* is the time to make several copies of your Career Analysis Form. You'll need these copies to evaluate all of the careers you're considering at this time. Make a few extra copies in case you decide to analyze additional careers in the future. At the top of each Career Analysis Form is a place for you to write in the specific career option that you'll be analyzing on that particular form. Write each of the career options you're considering at the top of the forms.

Step 4. Now determine how well each of the career options that you're considering relates to the values you've identified as important to your career decision. Go through each Career Analysis Form and determine how well each particular career option accommodates those values. Place your rating of the career for each value in the column labeled Career Score, using the following scale:

1	2	3	4	5	6	7	8	9	10

The Value Is Not Accommodated
by the Career at All

The Value Is Completely
Accommodated

Let's look at an example to illustrate this step of the process. Suppose that one of the career options I had identified for myself back in Chapter 5 was Movie Director. My Career Analysis Form for Movie Director might look something like this:

SPECIFIC CAREER OPTION: _Movie Director_			
Values	Value points	Career score	Weighted value
Time with family	30	3	
Flexible work schedule	15	6	
Stable income	10	4	
Opportunity for creativity	10	10	
Opportunity for promotion	7	9	
Social interaction	7	10	
Opportunity to write	7	8	
Health insurance	7	2	
Professional atmosphere	7	7	
		CAREER POINT TOTAL:	

The career points I assigned to Movie Director reflect my understanding of how well a career as a movie director accommodates those values that I consider critical to my career satisfaction and personal happiness. For example, based on the information that I've gathered, the job shadowing that I've completed, and my understanding of employment opportunities in movie directing, it seems to me that a career as a movie director would provide very little time for me to spend with my family. My rating of "3" for the value labeled "Time with family" reflects that awareness. My rating of "4" for the value labeled "Stable income" reflects my understanding that movie directors can't always count on stable work.

As you complete each Career Analysis Form, don't get discouraged if there are a few values for which you're unable to assign a Career Score right away because of lack of information. Even if you've spent many hours gathering information about your career options, it's common to discover that you aren't aware of all the important details associated with a particular career. Try calling someone you know who might have the information you need, or try to locate some of the resources discussed in Chapter 6. If you look hard enough, you'll be sure to discover the information sooner or later.

Step 5. This is the computational part of the exercise, in which you will determine Career Point Totals for each of the careers you're considering. This is accomplished in two stages. First, go through each Career Analysis Form and multiply the Value Points for each value by the Career Score you've assigned for that particular career. The resulting product is the Weighted Value. For example, on my Career Analysis Form for movie director, I assigned 30 Value Points to "Time with family" (as I did on all of my Career Analysis Forms) and a Career Score of 3 for that value as it relates to movie directing. Multiplying 30 by 3, I arrive at a score of 90. That number is placed in the fourth column (Weighted Value) of the Career Analysis Form.

After I multiply each line's Value Points by the Career Score, my Career Analysis Form for movie directing looks like this:

SPECIFIC CAREER OPTION: _Movie Director_

Values	Value points		Career score		Weighted value
Time with family	30	X	3	=	90
Flexible work schedule	15	X	6	=	90
Stable income	10	X	4	=	40
Opportunity for creativity	10	X	10	=	100
Opportunity for promotion	7	X	9	=	63
Social interaction	7	X	10	=	70
Opportunity to write	7	X	8	=	56
Health insurance	7	X	2	=	14
Professional atmosphere	7	X	7	=	49
			CAREER POINT TOTAL:		572

Finally, add up all of the scores in the fourth column for each Career Option you've analyzed. When I do this for movie director, my Career Point Total is 572.

Step 6. The final step of the Career Analysis System is to determine which career option has the highest Career Point Total, as this career will become your tentative career choice. Why? Because the career with the highest total points is the career option that best accommodates the values that you've identified as most important to you. As such, it's likely to provide you with the greatest degree of career satisfaction, employment stability, and job success. So that you can reach a sense of closure at this point in the career decision-making process, in the space below write in the career option that you've determined to be your tentative career choice *at this time:*

_____

Congratulations! You've made a tentative career decision based on a thorough analysis of your interests, skills, experiences, and values. You've analyzed the factors that matter to you most, and you've integrated all sorts of information into your decision. There's no doubt that you've made a career decision that counts!

SURFING THE WEB WITH A PURPOSE

www.nbcc.org/find/nccc.htm Although the process of finding a career counselor is described in other chapters of this book, doing so is especially relevant at this stage of the career decision-making process. This site, sponsored by the National Board for Certified Counselors (NBCC), includes an interactive feature by which you can contact NBCC officials to obtain a list of Nationally Certified Career Counselors in your area or region.

http://stats.bls.gov/asp/oep/noeted/empoptd.asp This is the Bureau of Labor Statistics' occupational employment, training, and earnings page. It can help you identify very important facts about careers you're still considering.

www.acinet.org/acinet/rsource/guides.htm This site, sponsored by America's Career InfoNet, offers numerous career assessments, as well as employment trends and projections, salary and wage surveys, and other work and life issues. The information you'll find here can help you determine which of two or three career alternatives seems most in line with your career self-concept.

QUESTIONS FOR CRITICAL THOUGHT

1. Why are career decisions made at this point in career development often referred to as *tentative* career decisions?
2. Why is career development considered a lifelong process?
3. Why is it important to evaluate tentative career decisions thoroughly before implementing them?
4. Why does the consideration of your work-related and core life values play such a prominent role in the completion of the Career Analysis Forms?

SPECIFIC CAREER OPTION: _____

Values	Value points	Career score	Weighted value
_____	_____	_____	_____
_____	_____	_____	_____
_____	_____	_____	_____
_____	_____	_____	_____
_____	_____	_____	_____
_____	_____	_____	_____
_____	_____	_____	_____
_____	_____	_____	_____
_____	_____	_____	_____
_____	_____	_____	_____
_____	_____	_____	_____
_____	_____	_____	_____
_____	_____	_____	_____
_____	_____	_____	_____
_____	_____	_____	_____
_____	_____	_____	_____
_____	_____	_____	_____
_____	_____	_____	_____
_____	_____	_____	_____
_____	_____	_____	_____
_____	_____	_____	_____
_____	_____	_____	_____

CAREER POINT TOTAL: _____

Lights, camera, action!

CREATING A CAREER ACTIVITIES TIMELINE

If we use the analogy of building a new home to describe the process of career development, then making a tentative career choice is a lot like finishing the foundation. A tentative career choice represents the culmination of a great deal of time and energy that has been invested in the career decision-making process. But like completing the foundation of a new home, this is certainly not the end of the process. In fact, in many ways it's only the beginning.

The purpose of this chapter is to assist you in the process of generating short-term goals and developing a detailed plan for carrying out your career decision. If there's one thing that counselors have learned over the years, it's that setting short-term goals increases our chances of realizing long-term goals. In this chapter, you'll have the opportunity to think about educational and training requirements, financial needs, and other important factors that will undoubtedly influence how successful you'll be at eventually achieving your career aspirations.

SETTING GOALS

Now that you've made a tentative decision of which career to pursue, it's time to make it happen! You need to think about several things if you want to implement your tentative career choice successfully. The first thing you need to do is determine the steps that are necessary for you to realize your goal.

The good news is that generating a list of steps probably won't require gathering much new information. If you've already adequately researched the career that you've selected to pursue, then you should already know the answers to most of the important questions. For example, the educational preparation or training required for entry into your career choice is something that you probably learned in Chapter 6 when you completed the Career Information and Job Shadow Evaluation Forms for your tentative career choices.

In addition to your knowledge of specific job preparation requirements, other important factors will also influence your career activities timeline. Making a career choice and carrying out that choice is probably not the *only* concern in your life right now—other aspects of your personal life certainly deserve your attention as well.

In Exercise 1.1 you thought about *all* of the things that you'd like to accomplish within the next 20 years or so. You may have listed goals that have little to do with making career decisions or accomplishing career-related tasks. As you think about implementing your career choice, remember to consider other factors in your life and how they're going to affect your ability to carry out the remaining stages of the career decision-making process. The last thing that you want to do is focus exclusively on career decision making at the expense of important interpersonal relationships and other responsibilities you have.

Consider all relevant factors in your life as you develop a timeline for carrying out your career goals.

The bottom line is this: Career development—despite its importance—is only one part of who you are. Spiritual, mental, emotional, and physical well-being are also extremely important facets in your life. Each contributes to your overall life satisfaction. Make sure that you consider all relevant factors as you develop a timeline for carrying out your career goals.

Consider how your career decisions will influence your family relationships. If you have significant others (e.g., children, a partner), remember that your career decisions will have a direct impact on their lives, too. Such persons should play an important role in clarifying your goals and determining helpful strategies for accomplishing them.

As with any goal-setting exercise, you need to develop a timeline that is realistic. Don't be too ambitious as you consider the length of time necessary to complete each of the steps required to realize your career goal. It's much better to set realistic goals, allowing yourself plenty of time to complete each task, rather than set up a timeline that leaves no room for unexpected events and challenges that might come your way.

CONSIDER   *Winnie*

Winnie, a college student I met with a couple of years ago, had experienced frustration and anxiety because of her inability to accomplish certain goals in the timeline that she had created for herself. Winnie was a 38-year-old, single mother of four children, and was attending college with plans of becoming an accountant. She had decided that she should be able to achieve her goal within five years. She believed that it shouldn't take her any longer than that, and she needed the increase in salary potential as soon as possible.

Like many of today's college students, Winnie was working full-time. On an average day, she got up at about 5:00 in the morning to take care of housework and to study for an hour or so. Then, after getting her kids off to school, Winnie went to work, where she stayed until 4:00 each afternoon. After working all day she went back home to feed her kids. Four nights a week she attended classes from 6:30 to 10:00 p.m.

It didn't take too long to understand why Winnie was experiencing a lot of frustration and anxiety. She was trying to accomplish something that may have been *theoretically* possible but that was placing great amounts of strain and stress on her personal life. Winnie and I worked on creating a more appropriate timeline that allowed her more flexibility and yet still kept her moving toward her career goal.

The moral of Winnie's story, like so many others that I've witnessed over the years, is that balance in life is a very good thing. It's better to develop a career goals timeline that takes into account other aspects of your life rather than one that assumes that career decision making is all that matters.

The first thing you need to do to create your tentative career timeline is make a list of the major tasks necessary to enter the career you've selected. These tasks usually include such things as selecting a major, identifying financial resources, completing course work, securing credentials or certifications, and obtaining a degree. If you've completed the exercises in Chapter 6, then you should have ready access to most of the information about educational and training requirements associated with your career choice.

EDUCATIONAL AND TRAINING OPPORTUNITIES

One of the most important factors in realizing your career goal involves obtaining required education and training. A variety of educational and training opportunities are available—some more appropriate than others, depending on the type of career you're pursuing. An overview of some of the more popular types of educational and training opportunities may help you consider which avenue is the most appropriate to pursue.

Vocational and Technical Schools

Vocational and technical schools are designed to provide students with job-specific training in specific fields of interest. Trade schools, technical institutes, and home-study or correspondence schools often fall into this category. Many people who are interested in gaining entry-level jobs in career fields as diverse as cosmetology, lock-smithing, truck driving, and computer repairing utilize vocational and technical school training in their career preparation.

The length of time required to complete vocational and technical school training can vary from a few months to a few years. Training usually involves practical classroom experience along with some traditional academics. Graduation from a vocational or technical school often results in a certificate of completion that graduates can use to obtain entry-level work in the field. Many employers also allow for some amount of on-the-job training upon hire.

Community and Junior Colleges

Some individuals attend community and junior colleges to take preparatory courses for obtaining a four-year degree. Most community and junior colleges offer a variety of courses that can be transferred as credit to most four-year institutions. Taking classes at community and junior colleges can be an excellent way to begin working on a four-year degree. Such courses usually cost less, have smaller class sizes, and are offered on a more flexible time schedule than courses offered at a large four-year college or university.

Many other students attend two-year programs at community or junior colleges to gain marketable skills preparatory to an entry-level career position. Many of the two-year associate degree programs offered at most community or junior colleges are similar to the training offered at vocational and technical schools. But community colleges also offer other expanded training programs, such as programs in nursing, drafting, and emergency medical technology.

Still other students attend community and junior colleges to engage in lifelong learning. Continuing education courses in a wide variety of career fields are usually offered at two-year colleges as an ongoing service to members of the community. Such courses might include computer software training, information on how to start your own business, or tips on completing your tax return.

Four-Year Colleges and Universities

Four-year colleges and universities are attended by persons whose career goals require at least a bachelor's degree. Students who attend such institutions will normally complete a general set of courses (usually referred to as general education or core curriculum requirements) in such subjects as history, English, and math, along with specialized courses directly associated with particular careers. Students "major" in one or two fields that serve as preparation for a career. They can also "minor" in related fields that can provide additional educational experiences related to a given career field.

Some careers require additional education beyond a bachelor's degree. Many professions, such as law, medicine, and psychology, require a master's or a doctoral degree for entry-level employment. The additional time required beyond a bachelor's degree to complete these programs varies from one or two years to six or seven and sometimes even more.

Apprenticeship Programs

On-the-job training with limited classroom instruction is provided by most apprenticeship programs. Labor unions usually sponsor such programs, although some are sponsored by actual employers or government agencies. A person who completes an apprenticeship program (which can last anywhere from a few months to several years) is generally considered a "qualified" professional in that particular field.

Apprenticeship programs are popular methods of training in many careers associated with construction work, mechanical repair, and industrial production. Automobile mechanics, carpenters, heating and air conditioning specialists, and electricians are examples of professionals who often receive their training through apprenticeship programs. You can find a directory of union organizations offering apprenticeships at www.igc.org/igc/ln/resources/unions.html.

The Armed Services

The armed forces can serve as an excellent training ground for individuals interested in a variety of careers. Positions in the armed services include the same types of jobs that civilians obtain, such as nursing, mechanics, and air traffic controlling. Many people join the army, air force, navy, marines, coast guard, or reserves as a way to gain valuable experience and master various job skills. Upon discharge from the armed services, many persons utilize the training they received as a springboard to other careers.

Several different training programs and educational options are available to persons interested in the armed services. You've probably heard about ROTC (Reserve Officers' Training Corps) programs and the GI bill, which can support the cost of an education at a college or university in return for service in a branch of the military. You might want to talk with a military recruiter if this option interests you.

If you have difficulty determining which type of educational or training opportunity is most appropriate for you, a career counselor or academic advisor may be able to point you in the right direction. Don't forget to utilize the information you gathered in Chapter 6, too. Sources such as O*NET, the OOH, and computer-assisted career information and guidance programs can help you decide which type of training or educational opportunity to consider.

FACTORS TO CONSIDER WHEN SELECTING A SCHOOL OR TRAINING PROGRAM

Once you've determined what type of educational or training program is best for you, you'll need to select an appropriate institution. Making that decision requires you to consider a variety of factors.

You should begin this process by identifying the institutions within your geographical limitations that offer the type of training you're in need of. If you're pursuing a career in automobile repair, for example, and you've decided to obtain an associate's degree in automotive technology from a community or junior college, then you'll want to determine which community and junior colleges you're able to attend. If you're pursuing a career that requires a bachelor's degree or additional academic credentials, then you'll want to take a look at the four-year colleges and universities that offer degree programs in your area of interest.

As you examine the various options available to you, consider how each institution measures up in terms of the following factors.

Tuition and Related Expenses

Obtaining adequate education and training can be quite a costly venture. Consider the cost of tuition as well as other costs associated with attending a particular institution, such as books, parking, transportation, supplies, and housing (if applicable).

Accreditation of the Institution

Most institutions are accredited in one way or another. Accreditation involves a group of professionals external to the institution making a determination regarding the quality of education or training offered at that particular site. A program of study or college that is accredited is one that has been "approved" by external reviewers.

Academic Calendar

Most colleges and universities conduct classes on either a quarter or semester system. Institutions that operate on the quarter system usually have four 10- or 12-week terms during the course of the year. Those that operate on the semester system usually offer classes in two 15- or 16-week terms and sometimes during the summer. Technical and vocational schools vary in their schedules but usually offer a variety of academic calendar options to meet the needs of students.

Requirements for Admission

Review the requirements for admission to an institution to make sure that you qualify. Grade-point averages from previous educational experiences (e.g., high school grades) and scores on standardized tests (e.g., the SAT or ACT) are usually considered along with letters of recommendation and a personal essay.

Length of Program

Training programs, especially those offered by an apprenticeship program or a technical or vocational training center, can vary dramatically in length. The length of time involved in securing the credentials or certificates necessary for you to pursue your career can be an important factor in your decision of where to obtain your training.

Financial Aid/Grants/Scholarships

Consider financial resources available to you for carrying out your career plan. These days, even one year of education can be extremely costly. Determining methods for funding your education or training is an important aspect of career planning that is often neglected. It's best to have an established plan for funding your career goals so that you don't find yourself without the resources to complete your training. Consider current funding sources as well as alternative sources that may be available to you in the future. Financial aid counselors at most colleges and universities can provide you with helpful information. They'll be able to project costs associated with attending college, and they'll inform you of local and national scholarships and grants for which you might qualify.

SELECTING A MAJOR

Once you've determined where you're going to obtain your educational training and experience, at some point you'll need to declare a major. Consulting a career counselor at the institution and talking with an advisor are two of the best ways to determine which major is appropriate for you given your particular career interests.

An advisor will be able to tell you the exact courses you'll need for completing a particular degree program as well as help you structure a timeline for accomplishing those tasks. If you've decided to seek a career as a chemist or a biologist, then the appropriate major is fairly obvious. But many careers, contrary to popular belief, don't necessarily require one particular academic course of study. Many law schools, for example, encourage prospective applicants to major in any one of a variety of disciplines, ranging from history and journalism to political science and biology. Medical schools accept applicants with a wide range of backgrounds and experience, including students with degrees in psychology, physics, and English—just to name a few.

The important thing is to meet with the persons who are likely to provide you with helpful advice. Career counselors, advisors, and people you know who are currently employed in the career you're pursuing are often very reliable sources of information.

Another resource you may want to consult as you think about declaring a major is the Prentice Hall Web site at www.prenhall.com/success. This site has an area on majors selection that many students I have worked with in the past have found very useful in identifying appropriate majors associated with particular career goals.

CONSIDER *Nick*

A few months ago I had the opportunity to work with Nick, a 19-year old community college student. Although he was only in his second semester of college-level studies, Nick had thoroughly engaged in the career exploration process. He had spent over 80 hours researching career options, job shadowing, and engaging in informational interviewing. As a result, he was very confident in his desire to become a medical doctor. He even set his sights on being admitted to the medical school at the University of California, Los Angeles (UCLA). What he didn't know, however, was what major would be most appropriate as a pre-med student.

I encouraged Nick to do several things to help determine what major (or majors) would be most appropriate for him to consider. First, Nick reviewed the information he had gathered earlier on in the career exploration process. This included a review of the information he found at the OOH Web site (http://stats.bls.gov/ocohome.htm), the data he gathered during the informational interviews he conducted, and advice he received during his job-shadowing experiences. Next, Nick corresponded (both by E-mail and by snail mail) with two different pre-med advisers at UCLA. The pre-med advisers provided Nick with a great deal of useful information. Not only did they inform Nick that the UCLA medical school accepted students with a variety of different undergraduate majors, but they also explained that in recent years the members of the UCLA medical school admissions committee were especially interested in admitting students with strong liberal arts backgrounds and majors outside of the more traditional biological or physical sciences.

Because Nick has a long-standing interest in anthropology, dating back to his middle school years, he talked with the UCLA pre-med advisors, several current medical school students, and to a couple of doctors in his home town about the idea of majoring in anthropology as a pre-med student. Each and every one of Nick's contacts thought that a major in anthropology sounded both exciting and appropriate, as long as he made sure to complete the requisite courses in biology, physics, chemistry, and mathematics.

CREATING A CAREER ACTIVITIES TIMELINE

As you make education and training decisions related to your career choice, you'll want to develop a timeline for completing the various steps involved in realizing your career goal. Think about the barriers you identified in Chapter 7 and make sure to allow ample time in your career plan for addressing them. It's all part of careful, realistic planning for your career.

You might want to go back and review your answers to Exercises 7.1 and 7.2 in preparation for completing Exercise 9.1, "Career Preparation Requirements," and Exercise 9.2, "Creating the Timeline."

CAREER PREPARATION REQUIREMENTS	**EXERCISE 9.1**

This exercise helps you organize the information you've gathered so that you'll be better able to construct a career timeline.

Step 1. Begin by noting the requirements associated with your tentative career choice. The example below illustrates how this is to be done.

Sample Career Preparation Requirements

TENTATIVE CAREER CHOICE: *Petroleum Engineer*

List below the educational and training requirements associated with your career choice:

EDUCATIONAL REQUIREMENTS

Completion of a bachelor's degree; major in engineering.

TRAINING REQUIREMENTS

Internship or cooperative learning experience at a petroleum company during my senior year.

LICENSURE/CERTIFICATION/CREDENTIALS REQUIREMENTS

Not applicable

ADDITIONAL REQUIREMENTS

Learn more about the petroleum industry.

Considering the other responsibilities in your life (in other words, making sure that you leave enough time to ensure that your personal needs are taken care of), how long do you think it'll take you to complete the educational and training requirements listed above?

Five years

Your Career Preparation Requirements

TENTATIVE CAREER CHOICE: _____

List below the educational and training requirements associated with your career choice:

EDUCATIONAL REQUIREMENTS

TRAINING REQUIREMENTS

LICENSURE/CERTIFICATION/CREDENTIALS REQUIREMENTS

ADDITIONAL REQUIREMENTS

Considering the other responsibilities in your life (in other words, making sure that you leave enough time to ensure that your personal needs are taken care of), how long do you think it'll take you to complete the educational and training requirements listed above?

Step 2. Once you've identified the major educational, training, or other certification requirements associated with your career goal, it will be important to consider each of the steps you'll need to accomplish along the way.

| Kyra | **CONSIDER** |

Kyra, a student I recently worked with, made a tentative career decision to become a pediatrician. In addition to completing a bachelor's degree and then successfully completing medical school, Kyra will have to pass the medical licensure exam in the state in which she decides to practice medicine. The steps toward accomplishing these tasks include determining an appropriate major, applying for admission to medical school, and so forth. As she considers the many steps along the way, keeping in mind ways to accomplish each step and the time that will be involved, Kyra might draft plans such as these:

STEP: _Select an appropriate major_

PLAN OF ACTION TO ACCOMPLISH THIS STEP

Meet with my academic advisor and talk with my daughter's pediatrician for some advice.

OTHER THINGS I NEED TO CONSIDER WHEN COMPLETING THIS STEP

My academic advisor is generally only available on Friday afternoons, and I work on Fridays. I'll have to get a day off in a couple of weeks or find out if I can make an individual appointment for some other day of the week.

APPROXIMATE TIME FOR COMPLETING THIS STEP

By the end of next week

STEP: _Apply for medical school_

PLAN OF ACTION TO ACCOMPLISH THIS STEP

Take the Medical College Admissions Test (MCAT) Preparation course; meet with the pre-med advisor to get application forms; take the MCAT.

OTHER THINGS I NEED TO CONSIDER WHEN COMPLETING THIS STEP

The pre-med advisor is available for drop-in appointments every morning until 11:00. I'll need to go by on Tuesday or Thursday to get the MCAT application forms.

APPROXIMATE TIME FOR COMPLETING THIS STEP

March or April of my junior year

Step 3. Based on the information you've been able to gather relevant to your career choice, list below the steps you'll need to take to accomplish the educational and training requirements you've identified. (Make additional copies of this form if necessary.)

STEP: _____

PLAN OF ACTION TO ACCOMPLISH THIS STEP

_____

_____

_____

OTHER THINGS I NEED TO CONSIDER WHEN COMPLETING THIS STEP

_____

_____

_____

APPROXIMATE TIME FOR COMPLETING THIS STEP

_____

STEP: _____

PLAN OF ACTION TO ACCOMPLISH THIS STEP

_____

_____

_____

OTHER THINGS I NEED TO CONSIDER WHEN COMPLETING THIS STEP

_____

_____

_____

APPROXIMATE TIME FOR COMPLETING THIS STEP

_____

STEP: _____

PLAN OF ACTION TO ACCOMPLISH THIS STEP

_____

_____

_____

OTHER THINGS I NEED TO CONSIDER WHEN COMPLETING THIS STEP

_____

_____

_____

APPROXIMATE TIME FOR COMPLETING THIS STEP

_____

Before developing a timeline for accomplishing each of the steps you've identified, you may want to review the goal-setting guidelines summarized in the box below.

Factors to Consider When Creating Your Career Activities Timeline

Be Realistic

It doesn't make sense to create an overly ambitious timeline. Doing so only sets up a situation that tends to foster frustration and anxiety.

Create Balance

Don't forget the many responsibilities in your life. You'll need to address these areas of your life as you pursue your career goals. Be sure to leave ample time to devote to these personal issues.

Ask Others to Share Their Perspectives

The social network you've established can be a great source of advice and support during the career decision-making process. As you consider a timeline for completing the many tasks related to your career choice, these people can be very helpful to you.

Remember That This Timeline Is Tentative

No matter how organized we are, sometimes circumstances alter our plans. Allow yourself the flexibility to make changes to your timeline just in case the need arises.

Your Tentative Career Timeline

As you review the work you completed in Exercise 9.1, you should be able to place the specific tasks you need to accomplish into one of the time frames shown below.

TODAY'S DATE: _____

CAREER-RELATED TASKS TO ACCOMPLISH WITHIN THE NEXT FIVE TO TEN YEARS

Task   Completion Goal Date

_____   _____

_____   _____

_____   _____

_____   _____

_____   _____

CAREER-RELATED TASKS TO ACCOMPLISH WITHIN THE NEXT THREE TO FIVE YEARS

Task   Completion Goal Date

_____   _____

_____   _____

_____   _____

_____   _____

_____   _____

CAREER-RELATED TASKS TO ACCOMPLISH WITHIN THE NEXT TWO TO THREE YEARS

Task   Completion Goal Date

_____   _____

_____   _____

_____   _____

_____   _____

_____   _____

CAREER-RELATED TASKS TO ACCOMPLISH WITHIN THE NEXT SIX MONTHS TO A YEAR

Task   Completion Goal Date

_____   _____

_____   _____

_____   _____

_____   _____

_____   _____

CAREER-RELATED TASKS TO ACCOMPLISH WITHIN THE NEXT THREE TO SIX MONTHS

Task   Completion Goal Date

_____   _____

_____   _____

_____   _____

_____   _____

_____   _____

CAREER-RELATED TASKS TO ACCOMPLISH WITHIN THE NEXT TWO TO THREE MONTHS

Task   Completion Goal Date

_____   _____

_____   _____

_____   _____

_____   _____

_____   _____

CAREER-RELATED TASKS TO ACCOMPLISH WITHIN THE NEXT MONTH

Task   Completion Goal Date

_____   _____

_____   _____

_____   _____

_____   _____

Because goal-setting is such an important part of career decision making, make sure that you periodically review your list of goals and the tentative timeline you've developed. As you review your progress on a regular basis, you'll be able to refine your goals as necessary and develop new strategies for accomplishing the important tasks you've identified.

SURFING THE WEB WITH A PURPOSE

www.coun.uvic.ca/learn/program/hndouts/goals.html Part of the University of Victoria's Learning Skills Program, this Web site offers a motivation and goal-setting worksheet that will help you identify short- and long-term goals and develop a plan of action for achieving those goals. A nice feature of this site is a discussion of the consequences that follow the achievement of one or more of your goals.

www.militarycareers.com/ As you might have guessed, this is the home page for the military's career guide. One of the most useful features of this site is the ability to search for military opportunities on the basis of several different factors.

www.quintcareers.com/choosing_major.html Dr. Randall Hansen presents his views about choosing a college major at this Web site. His essay includes a summary of the career decision-making process, resources available to you as you begin to identify an appropriate college major, a number of books that you might consult when declaring a major, and a set of links to other useful Web sites that deal with choosing a college major.

www.uncwil.edu/stuaff/career/majors.htm Have you ever wondered what occupational opportunities exist for persons who major in Spanish or anthropology? Or perhaps you've always wondered what a degree in philosophy, religion, or geology prepares students to be able to do in the world of work. This Web site, sponsored by the University of North Carolina at Wilmington, provides an answer to the question, "What can I do with a major in . . . ?" for more than 40 different academic majors.

QUESTIONS FOR CRITICAL THOUGHT

1. What factors in your life should you consider as you develop short- and long-term career goals?
2. How can you ensure that your career goals are realistic?
3. Why is it helpful to consult with a career counselor or academic advisor when selecting an academic major?
4. What factors are important to consider as you create your career activities timeline?

What next?

10

As you firm up your tentative career choice and complete the steps that will allow you to fully realize your career goals, you'll find yourself completing the exploration stage of career development and entering the establishment stage. Although the focus of this book is on the exploration stage of the career decision-making process, this concluding chapter will provide an overview of the activities involved in the establishment, maintenance, and disengagement phases of career decision making and to discuss ways you might modify the career exploration process to fit your own individual needs.

ESTABLISHMENT AND MAINTENANCE STAGES OF CAREER DEVELOPMENT

One of the first things you'll do as you become established within a career is learn about the intricacies of that career. I've been working as a career counselor for many years, but that doesn't mean that I've learned *everything* there is to know about being a career counselor. I'm constantly learning new things and understanding concepts in greater depth.

During the establishment and maintenance stages of career development, you'll seek opportunities and learn strategies for enhancing your job satisfaction and happiness. This may mean preparing for promotions and job advancement or making a minor career change, such as looking for a supervisory position in the same career field or updating your skills to remain marketable in your chosen career.

Once you become established within a particular career field, it's a good idea to periodically evaluate your level of job satisfaction. One way to do this is to make a list of the pros and cons of your job. Another way involves completing some sort of job satisfaction survey or questionnaire. One of the most effective tools for evaluating your job satisfaction is the recently developed on-line version of the Optimization Inventory (available at www.actionsforsuccess.com). Another way to evaluate your current job satisfaction, or to predict the degree to which a particular employment opportunity might contribute to your satisfaction, is to complete the exercise you'll find in Appendix E of this book.

CONSIDER   *Linda*

Linda, a client I worked with several years ago, had been working in the banking industry for almost 20 years. She was generally satisfied with her career, but she wanted
to find out if there were ways that she could use her talents and skills to begin an
entrepreneurial activity. Linda knew that one day she would like to own a small business,
and she was beginning to wonder if the time was right.

Linda was in the maintenance stage of career development, but she wanted to create
some new challenges to keep her level of work motivation high and maintain a high level
of career satisfaction and success.

There's almost always some way to improve your work situation and career satisfaction.

Evaluating your career choice periodically by determining your current level of job satisfaction is a very good idea. There's almost always something that can be done to improve your work situation and, in turn, your career satisfaction. Seeking ways to improve your work situation should be an ongoing process as you begin to realize that career decision making is a lifelong process.

THE DISENGAGEMENT STAGE OF CAREER DEVELOPMENT

According to Dr. Super, the fifth and final stage of career development is *disengagement*. It's during disengagement that we begin to prepare for a complete change in our career. For some people disengagement from a career may mean making a major career change, such as moving from a career as an electrical engineer to a career as a math teacher. For most of us, however, disengagement simply means retirement. Though the focus of this book is on the exploration stage of career decision making, there are a few things about disengagement that you ought to know.

Probably the most important piece of advice regarding disengagement is: PREPARE!

The time to prepare for retirement is *now*. It's *never* too early to begin thinking about financial security, emotional stability, physical well-being, and leisure interests. The time to figure out what types of financial plans are available for retirement is now. The time to develop hobbies and leisure interests is now. The time to take care of physical needs by eating healthfully and staying in shape is now. Whether you're wrapping up the exploration stage of career decision making, establishing yourself within a selected career, entering the maintenance stage, or getting ready to retire, preparation is the key.

REFINING THE CAREER DECISION-MAKING PROCESS TO MEET YOUR NEEDS

Dr. Super's model of career development has been useful for many persons who have engaged in the career decision-making process, but that doesn't mean that it applies perfectly to everyone. Some persons need additional exploration activities before they're comfortable making a career choice. Others may simply take more time than average to complete all of the activities associated with the career decision-making process. You may need to adapt Dr. Super's model of career development to fit your particular life circumstances.

As you reflect on the career decision-making process, think about the steps that have worked particularly well for you. Perhaps the self-assessments of interests and skills in Chapter 3 played an important role in narrowing your career options. Or maybe the increased self-awareness you gained by exploring your values in Chapter 4 helped you reach a tentative decision you're pleased with. Then again, you may have found the list of resources in Chapter 6 for collecting information about occupations one of the most helpful components of the process. If you're able to determine which parts of this book have worked especially well for you, then you'll know the types of activities and exercises to complete again in the future.

As time goes on, think about the steps in the career decision-making process that have worked well for you.

As mentioned several times throughout this book, most everyone recycles through the career decision-making process at least a couple of times. If you're aware of which exercises are particularly helpful to you, then you'll know which parts of the book to revisit in the future when you are considering a career change.

Reynaldo

CONSIDER

Reynaldo was 42 years old and had worked for a large aluminum recycling factory since graduating from college with a degree in engineering at age 24. He had been successful in his job and had received a series of promotions over the years. Eventually Reynaldo was promoted to the position of Assistant Director of Research and Development. All seemed to be going well for Reynaldo—until he was laid off along with many other mid-level managers. After 18 years of steady work, Reynaldo found himself unemployed.

When Reynaldo and I met, one of the first things I recognized about him was that he was very satisfied working in the aluminum industry. He recounted several instances in the past in which he had received job offers to work somewhere else but declined those opportunities because he enjoyed his work so much. Now unemployed, Reynaldo explained to me that he wanted to find a new job that would be as similar to the one he had become accustomed to as possible.

There was certainly no need for Reynaldo to evaluate his interests and abilities or reflect on his values. Most of the exercises in Chapters 3 and 4, although essential for *most* people, would not have been the proper place for Reynaldo to begin. Reynaldo was keenly aware of the important aspects of his self-concept. So, the focus of our work together was targeted on the latter stages of the exploration process.

Because it had been so long since Reynaldo had applied for a job, we spent some time working on a resume and discussing important strategies to consider when completing job applications. We engaged in practice interviews and discussed methods for locating job openings for individuals with a background in engineering and recycling. In other words, we focused in on those activities that were likely to benefit Reynaldo most directly.

Because of the time we spent on these tasks, Reynaldo was able to obtain a satisfying new position as the Director of Training and Development with a large recycling company in a neighboring town.

Each of us has unique characteristics that influence our career decisions. When the time comes for you to recycle through the career decision-making process, which you'll undoubtedly do at some point in your life, you'll need to recognize which stages apply to your particular situation. Recycling may not require completion of each and every activity in this book. Instead, there may be a few chapters and exercises that apply to your situation. It will be up to you to deter-

Our unique characteristics influence our career decisions.

mine which parts of the book will be most beneficial to you. Rereading Chapter 2 and completing Exercise 2.1 again will always be a good place to start. It's a good way to figure out, at *any* point in time, which sections of the book apply most directly to your situation.

CONCLUSION

My primary hope in writing this book has been to impart to you the important things to consider when making career decisions and to show you how to engage in the career decision-making process in an effective and satisfying manner.

In particular, I hope you've learned

- That making career decisions requires a comprehensive understanding of who you are—what Dr. Super referred to as your self-concept.
- How critical it is that you have a good understanding of your personality, interests, skills, experiences, and values.
- How to integrate all aspects of your self-concept when making career decisions, thus maximizing your chances of career satisfaction and success.
- Valuable ways of thinking about potential barriers to your career choice.
- Methods for overcoming potential barriers.

Most of all, I hope you've experienced firsthand the fact that investing time and energy in the career decision-making process is well worth the effort.

Throughout this book you have gained tools that will assist you in making career decisions. Utilize those tools, invest yourself in the process, and you'll be sure to reap the benefits. Our careers are an integral part of who we are. Make sure that you do all that you can to maximize your chances of career satisfaction and success. If you do, you'll be sure to make career decisions that count!

SURFING THE WEB WITH A PURPOSE

http://findarticles.com/m3161/n19_v46/21114701/p1/article.jhtml At this site you will find an article by Lisa Hochgraf entitled, "Boosting Job Satisfaction by Defining and Pursuing Worklife Happiness." The article discusses steps you can engage in to increase your job satisfaction by defining your job needs.

www.redmole.co.uk/js_questionnaire/ This interactive job satisfaction questionnaire can be a useful tool for evaluating the degree to which you are satisfied with your current employment situation. Results of this inventory help to illuminate why it is that you might be considering a change in career or retirement from work altogether.

www.smartbiz.com/sbs/arts/bly64.htm This site includes a nicely written essay by Robert W. Bly on the topic of job burnout.

www.aarp.org With thousands of Web sites focusing on issues associated with retirement, it only makes sense to access the most popular site of them all. The American Association of Retired Person's home page includes multiple links to useful Internet resources, a copy of the latest AARP bulletin, and information about the association's benefits to members.

QUESTIONS FOR CRITICAL THOUGHT

1. How can you begin *now* to prepare for the latter stages of career development?
2. Why don't all stages of career exploration and planning apply uniformly to everyone?
3. Why is *recycling* such a common experience among today's workforce?
4. How can you determine which aspects of the career decision-making process are pertinent to you at any given point in time?

Appendix A

ENFJ

Religiously Oriented Occupations
Home Economist
Optometrist
Musician or Composer
Counselor
Artist or Entertainer
Dental Hygienist
Physician: Family, General Practice
Designer
Child Care Worker

ENFP

Counselor or Psychologist
Teacher: Arts, Health, Special
 Education
Researcher
Religiously Oriented Occupations
Writer or Editor
Musician or Composer
Social Scientist
Computer Professional
Public Relations Worker
Administrator: Education

ENTJ

Consultant: Management
Human Resources
Computer Professional
Physician: Family
Manager: Sales
Manager: Executive
Credit Investigator or Mortgage Broker
Marketing Professional
Administrator: Education
Administrator: Health

ENTP

Photographer
Marketing Professional
Writer or Journalist
Computer Professional
Credit Investigator or Mortgage
 Broker
Psychiatrist
Engineer
Construction Worker
Artist or Entertainer
Research Worker

ESFJ

Teacher
Administrator: Student Personnel
Manager: Office
Religiously Oriented Occupations
Dental Assistant
Child Care Worker
Home Economist
Hairdresser or Cosmetologist
Receptionist
Food Service Worker

ESFP

Child Care Worker
Teacher
Designer
Receptionist
Transportation Worker
Factory Supervisor
Library Worker
Cashier
Lifeguard or Recreation Attendant
Food Service Worker

ESTJ

Manager: Small Business, Factory, Sales
Purchasing Agent
Teacher: Trade or Technical
Law Enforcement Worker
Factory Supervisor
Public Service or Community Health Worker
Cleaning Service Worker
School Bus Driver
Insurance Agent or Broker
Social Services Worker

ESTP

Marketing Professional
Law Enforcement Worker
Carpenter
Manager: Small Business or Government
Auditor
Craft Worker
Farmer
Laborer
Transportation Worker
Factory Worker

INFJ

Religiously Oriented Occupations
Counselor, Psychologist, or Social Worker
Psychiatrist
Teacher
Consultant: Education
Doctor or Nurse
Architect
Fine Artist
Research Assistant
Marketing Professional

INFP

Artist or Entertainer
Psychiatrist
Counselor, Psychologist, or Social Worker
Architect
Research Assistant
Social Scientist
Writer or Editor
Laboratory Technologist
Consultant: Education
Therapist: Physical

INTJ

Architect
Computer Professional
Consultant: Management
Manager: Executive
Human Resources Personnel
Lawyer or Judge
Research Worker
Social Services Worker
Engineer
Scientist: Life or Physical

INTP

Computer Professional
Architect
Research Assistant
Fine Artist
Food Service Worker
Surveyor
Manager: Executive
Social Scientist
Writer or Editor
Photographer

ISFJ

Nursing
Teacher
Religiously Oriented Occupations
Administrator: Social Services
Librarian
Physician: Family, General Practice
Health Service Worker
School Bus Driver
Food Service
Private Household Worker

ISFP

Nurse
Storekeeper
Law Enforcement Worker
Carpenter
Surveyor
Clerical Supervisor
Dental Assistant
Bookkeeper
Cleaning Service Worker
Cook

ISTJ

Manager: Small Business, Factory
Accountant
Manager: Executive
Law Enforcement Worker
School Principal
School Bus Driver
Purchasing Agent
Computer Professional
Dentist
Steelworker

ISTP

Farmer
Military Officer or Enlistee
Engineer
Law Enforcement Worker
Engineering or Science Technician
Coal Miner
Transportation Worker
Dental Assistant
Laborer
Mechanic

Appendix B

EXERCISE 3.1: What's My Type? (Pages 28–30) and

EXERCISE 3.2: Career Dreaming (Page 31)

To score Exercises 3.1 and 3.2, you'll need to determine which "work environment" best describes each of the careers included on your list. "Work environment" refers to Dr. Roe's categories for describing career types: Service, Business Contact, Organization, Technology, Outdoors, Science, General Culture, and Arts and Entertainment. Refer to Table 1.1 on page 4 for Dr. Roe's classification system.

Next to each of the careers included in your lists on pages 30 and 31, write the work environment type that *best* describes that particular career. If you're unable to determine which work environment is most appropriate for a particular career, you might ask a career counselor or teacher for some advice or consult Appendix C for a list of careers arranged by occupational type.

An example might help to clarify this scoring procedure. One of the careers I would probably include on my Dream List would be "actor." Because being an actor involves artistic talent and creativity, and because the description of the Arts and Entertainment work environment is the best description of the types of things an actor is involved in, I would write ARTS AND ENTERTAINMENT next to "actor." Another career I would include on my Dream List would be pediatrician. If I looked at Table 1.1 and was not sure which work environment is associated with being a pediatrician, then I could turn to Appendix C. Referring to Appendix C, I'd discover that the appropriate occupational type for pediatrician is Science. If you're unable to figure out the appropriate career type for a particular career you're considering, ask an instructor, career counselor, or adviser for some guidance.

Go ahead now and write on pages 30 and 31 the primary occupational type (Service, Business Contact, Organization, Technology, Outdoors, Science, General Culture, or Arts and Entertainment) next to each of the careers in your lists from Exercises 3.1 and 3.2.

Next, fill in the "scores" for each work environment category by awarding 5 points for each occurrence of the occupational types included in your lists. For example, if my list of careers generated from Exercise 3.1 included one Arts and

Entertainment career, four Service careers, and three Science careers, then I would award 5 points to Arts and Entertainment (because my list included one Arts and Entertainment career), 20 points to Service, and 15 points to Science. My scores for this exercise would look like this:

SCORES FROM EXERCISE 3.1

Service	Business Contact	Organization	Technology	Outdoors	Science	General Culture	Arts & Entertainment
20	0	0	0	0	15	0	5

Repeat this process for assigning scores to each of the career types for Exercise 3.2.

EXERCISE 3.3: Activities Ratings (Page 32)

This exercise also results in a score for each of the work environments. The total score for each type is determined by adding together the ratings you assigned to each of the activities representing a particular occupational type. Your Service score, for example, is the sum of your ratings for the five Service types of activities included in Exercise 3.3.

The guide shown below indicates which items in Exercise 3.3 represent each work environment. For example, item numbers 5, 8, 26, 32, and 39 represent service careers. Above each item number, fill in the ratings you gave the item in Exercise 3.3. Then simply add up your scores in each occupational category to determine your total scores. Each total score should be somewhere between 5 and 25 points. Place the score for each career type in the appropriate spaces in Exercise 5.1 (p. 49).

SERVICE:

_____ + _____ + _____ + _____ + _____ = _____
 5   8   26   32   39

BUSINESS CONTACT:

_____ + _____ + _____ + _____ + _____ = _____
 2   12   24   33   36

ORGANIZATION:

_____ + _____ + _____ + _____ + _____ = _____
 3   11   14   18   22

TECHNOLOGY:

_____ + _____ + _____ + _____ + _____ = _____
 15   21   27   35   40

OUTDOORS:

_____ + _____ + _____ + _____ + _____ = _____
 6   10   16   30   38

SCIENCE:

_____ + _____ + _____ + _____ + _____ = _____
 1   7   17   20   25

GENERAL CULTURE:

_____ + _____ + _____ + _____ + _____ = _____
 4   13   19   29   37

ARTS AND ENTERTAINMENT:

_____ + _____ + _____ + _____ + _____ = _____
 9   23   28   31   34

Exercise 3.4: Linking the Past to the Present (Page 34)

To score this exercise, follow the same procedure as for scoring Exercise 3.3. The guide shown below indicates which items in Exercise 3.4 represent each career type. As you did for Exercise 3.3, add up the ratings for each type and record them in the appropriate spaces in Exercise 5.1.

SERVICE:

_____ + _____ + _____ + _____ + _____ = _____
  2   10   17   25   36

BUSINESS CONTACT:

_____ + _____ + _____ + _____ + _____ = _____
  3   13   23   28   37

ORGANIZATION:

_____ + _____ + _____ + _____ + _____ = _____
  7   20   24   29   35

TECHNOLOGY:

_____ + _____ + _____ + _____ + _____ = _____
  6   21   26   34   38

OUTDOORS:

_____ + _____ + _____ + _____ + _____ = _____
  4   12   15   30   39

SCIENCE:

_____ + _____ + _____ + _____ + _____ = _____
  5   11   18   22   32

GENERAL CULTURE:

_____ + _____ + _____ + _____ + _____ = _____
  8   16   27   31   40

ARTS AND ENTERTAINMENT:

_____ + _____ + _____ + _____ + _____ = _____
  1   9   14   19   33

Exercise 3.5: How Well Do You Do What You Do? (Page 35)

As you did for Exercises 3.3 and 3.4, you simply need to determine the total rating points for the skills representing each career type. The guide shown below indicates which skill items in Exercise 3.5 represent each career type. Record the total scores for each type in the appropriate spaces in Exercise 5.1.

SERVICE:

_____ + _____ + _____ + _____ + _____ = _____
 1   13   17   23   30

BUSINESS CONTACT:

_____ + _____ + _____ + _____ + _____ = _____
 5   15   25   35   39

ORGANIZATION:

_____ + _____ + _____ + _____ + _____ = _____
 4   9   16   20   29

TECHNOLOGY:

_____ + _____ + _____ + _____ + _____ = _____
 10   18   26   33   37

OUTDOORS:

_____ + _____ + _____ + _____ + _____ = _____
 2   8   24   31   38

SCIENCE:

_____ + _____ + _____ + _____ + _____ = _____
 12   21   27   32   36

GENERAL CULTURE:

_____ + _____ + _____ + _____ + _____ = _____
 3   7   19   22   28

ARTS AND ENTERTAINMENT:

_____ + _____ + _____ + _____ + _____ = _____
 6   11   14   34   40

Appendix C

Service

Barber
Bartender
Career counselor
Chef
Child care worker
Clinical psychologist
Correctional officer
Counseling psychologist
Counselor (general)
Day care worker
Dental assistant
Detective
Dietician/nutritionist
Emergency medical technician
FBI agent
Firefighter
Flight attendant
Food service worker
Hairdresser

Highway patrol officer
Homemaker
Hospital attendant
Lifeguard
Occupational therapist
Physical therapist
Police officer
Police sergeant
Practical nurse
Prison guard
Probation officer
Psychotherapist
Religious worker
Server (restaurant)
Sheriff
Social worker
Taxi driver
Teacher's aide
YMCA/YWCA director

Business Contact

Advertising executive
Auctioneer
Automobile salesperson
Insurance salesperson
Insurance agent/broker
Marketing professional
Mortgage broker

Promoter
Public relations specialist
Real estate agent
Retail/wholesale dealer
Sales representative
Traveling salesperson

Organization

Accountant
Actuary
Administrative assistant
Armed services officer
Auditor
Banker
Bank teller
Bookkeeper
Business executive
Business manager
Buyer
Cashier
Certified public accountant
Chief executive officer
Clerical supervisor
Court reporter
Department store clerk
Employment manager
Financial manager
Financial planner
General office clerk
Government executive
Health administrator
Hotel clerk
Hotel manager

Human resources director
Management consultant
Medical records technician
Office clerk
Office manager
Payroll clerk
Personnel manager
Politician
Postal worker
Public official
Purchasing agent
Receptionist
Restaurant manager
Retail sales manager
Sales clerk
Sales manager
Secretary
Shipping and receiving clerk
Small business owner
Statistician
Stenographer
Stockbroker
Typist
Warehouse supervisor
Word processing specialist

Technology

Aerospace engineer
Aircraft mechanic
Applied scientist
Auto body repairer
Automobile mechanic
Aviator/pilot
Bricklayer
Building contractor
Bus driver
Butcher
Carpenter
Chemical engineer
Civil engineer
Computer repairer
Construction worker

Draftsperson
Electrician
Electronics equipment repairer
Engineer (general)
Engineering technician
Engine mechanic
Factory worker
Farm equipment mechanic
General repairperson
Heating, air conditioning, and refrigeration technician
Heavy equipment specialist
Jeweler
Machinist
Mechanic

Technology (continued)

Mechanical engineer

Painter

Pipefitter

Plumber

Printer

Printing press operator

Sheet metal worker

Steel worker

Tailor

Truck driver

Welder

Outdoors

Agricultural specialist

Agronomist

Botanist

Dairy hand

Farmer

Floriculturalist

Forest ranger

Game warden

Gardener

Horticulturalist

Landscape architect

Land surveyor

Rancher

Tractor driver

Tree surgeon

Wildlife specialist

Science

Anthropologist

Archaeologist

Astronomer

Audiologist

Biochemist

Biologist

Cardiologist

Chemist

Chiropractor

Dentist

Experimental psychologist

Laboratory technician

Life scientist

Mathematician

Medical specialist

Medical technician

Meteorologist

Neurologist

Nurse

Obstetrician

Oceanographer

Ophthalmologist

Optometrist

Paleontologist

Pathologist

Pediatrician

Pharmacist

Physician

Physicist

Podiatrist

Psychiatrist

Psychologist

Radiologist

Research scientist

Science teacher

Sociologist

Speech pathologist

Surgeon

University/college professor (science field)

Veterinarian

X-ray technician

General Culture

Broadcaster

Clergy (minister, rabbi, priest)

Editor

Educational administrator

Elementary school teacher

High school teacher

Historian

Interpreter

Journalist

Judge

Law clerk

Lawyer

Librarian

Newscaster

News commentator

Paralegal assistant

Philosopher

Preschool teacher

Radio announcer

Reporter

School principal

School superintendent

Social scientist

Teacher

University/college professor

Urban planner

Arts and Entertainment

Actor

Advertising artist

Advertising writer

Architect

Art teacher

Art critic

Artist

Athletic coach

Author/writer

Choreographer

Cinematographer

Commercial artist

Composer

Cosmetologist

Dance instructor

Dancer

Designer

Drama teacher

Entertainer

Fine artist

Graphic designer

Interior decorator

Music arranger

Musician

Performing artist

Photographer

Professional athlete

Race car driver

Screenwriter

Sculptor

Singer

Stage designer

Appendix D

Probably the most important thing to remember about job search strategies is that the more strategies you're willing to use, the better your chances are for locating the type of job you really want. By expanding your job search strategies to include multiple sources, you increase your chances of finding out about a significantly greater number of jobs. The following list provides you with information about several resources available to help you when seeking part-time, volunteer, or full-time employment.

CLASSIFIED ADVERTISEMENTS

Many people find out about job openings by reading the classified ads in their local newspapers. In large towns, there are often hundreds and sometimes thousands of jobs in a variety of fields listed in each week's Sunday paper. These job opportunities are arranged alphabetically by job type and can provide you with a quick reference to job openings in your area. Even in smaller towns, many job openings are listed in the classified ads. If you're hoping to work somewhere other than where you're currently living, then you should check the classified ads of the newspaper published in that particular city.

With the advent of the Internet, many newspapers now provide on-line access to the most recent classified ads section of their paper. If you're not sure whether your city's newspaper is accessible via the Web, try calling the newspaper's editorial offices or using a search engine to search for your city's newspaper. Remember that classified job listings represent only a very small percentage of existing job openings. That's why you'll want to use a variety of other resources when searching for a job.

YOUR NETWORK OF CONNECTIONS

These days, with increased competition for jobs, many people are realizing that their personal and professional connections often play an important role in securing a job. The more people you know who are willing to help you locate the type of job you're seeking, the better off you'll be. The time to begin making these connections is now—well before you're ready to begin working full-time in your selected career field. Your network of connections can include personal friends, family members, community and religious leaders, and other persons who can help you locate potential openings in your field.

TEACHERS AND COUNSELORS

High school teachers and college professors who are actively involved in their communities are often valuable sources for identifying employment opportunities related to your selected career. You might try asking some of your teachers for information they have about job openings in your area. At the very least, they may be able to point you in certain directions that will increase your chances of finding a good job. Career counselors can also be a helpful source of information about employment opportunities. In addition to offering the same type of help teachers and professors can provide, career counselors—especially those who work at college and university career centers—often receive job announcements. Check with your college or university career center to find out if such announcements are available at your career center and whether or not they're accessible on-line.

JOB POSTINGS

Many jobs that are available in a community are included in job postings, lists of jobs that are available (often in both hard copy and via the Internet) within a company or an organization. Most college and university career planning and placement centers post jobs in cabinets or on bulletin boards so that you can quickly see what opportunities are available both on and off campus. Many large companies also list current openings in weekly or bi-weekly job bulletins. These bulletins usually consist of a printout of current jobs for which the company is accepting applications. You might want to make a quick phone call to the human resources directors of organizations that interest you and ask for the latest copy of their job bulletin.

TELEPHONE JOB LISTINGS

To cut down on the costs associated with advertising job openings, many companies—including most state and local governments—have developed telephone "hot lines." These hot lines usually list all openings at a company or organization, informing prospective applicants of important information such as salary range and educational requirements. These hot lines are sometimes listed in the yellow pages. You can find out if a certain company operates a job hot line by calling the human resources department of that company or accessing the company's Web site.

CAREER FAIRS

Career fairs are large organized gatherings of several employers who are looking for new employees to join their companies. These fairs are usually organized by high schools, colleges, and universities or by large civic and community groups. In large cities, newspapers often sponsor career fairs as well. Career fairs are a good way to find out which companies are hiring in your area and what opportunities exist in other regions of the country. If you decide to attend a career fair, make sure that you dress appropriately and take copies of your resume along: You never know when someone you meet at a career fair might become a prospective employer.

COMPUTER NETWORK JOB LISTINGS

With the advent of the Internet and other computer network systems, it has become possible for you to find out about national and even international job opportunities related to your career choice in a matter of seconds. If you have access to the Internet, you might try looking at some of the more popular job search sites: www.monster.com, www.headhunter.net, www.hotjobs.com, www.ajb.org. These sites range in their content and appearance, but nearly all of them give you the opportunity to access job listings on the basis of a number of different factors (e.g., type of work, salary, geographic location).

ONE-STOP CAREER CENTERS

Because of the focus on school-to-work transitions in recent years, many county and state government agencies have established "one-stop career centers." One-stop career centers are designed to help members of the community with all stages of the career decision-making process. The focus of such centers, however, is usually to assist individuals who are looking for jobs in the area. Check to see if there is a one-stop career center in your community. Just about any college or university career center should be able to tell you whether or not one is available in your area.

EMPLOYMENT AGENCIES

Although at one time employment agencies and "headhunters" were one of the most commonly utilized sources for finding a job, these organizations are used much less nowadays. Nevertheless, you might want to find out if an employment agency can help you locate job openings related to your career choice. Keep in mind, however, that some employment agencies charge a fee for their services, whereas most of the other sources listed in this chapter are free of charge. Employment agencies are almost always listed in the yellow pages under "Employment." You might also want to consider talking with a temporary employment agency. What many people don't realize is that temporary agencies often help people find long-term, full-time employment. Furthermore, temporary situations often turn into permanent ones.

JOB APPLICATION PROCEDURES

Different jobs require different application procedures. Be sure to follow all application guidelines *strictly*. If an employer states in an advertisement for a position that resumes should be sent and that no phone calls will be accepted, then you should send your resume (along with a cover letter, of course) and *not* call the company. Although following directions may seem like common sense, I've had many clients over the years tell me that they always thought it would be a good idea to call the company anyway—even though the advertisement for the position said only to send a resume. Think about it for a moment: If you were an employer, would you want to hire someone who followed directions, or someone who decided to do it some other way instead?

Most jobs require prospective employees to complete an application form. If you have the opportunity to complete an application at home, then by all means do so. If you have access to a typewriter, the application should definitely be typed. If a typewriter isn't available, then at least *very neatly* print all of your information. If you must complete the application on site, then you should use a ball-point pen (blue or black ink) unless otherwise directed. Be sure to take your time to complete the information neatly and accurately. It's also a good idea to dress appropriately when completing an application on site, even if a job interview won't be conducted at that time. The first impression you make is often a lasting one.

Be sure you have all of the necessary information with you in case you have to complete applications on site. Take a copy of your resume with you. Information that is routinely requested on job applications is listed below.

Job Application Information

YOUR NAME, MAILING ADDRESS, TELEPHONE NUMBER, AND E-MAIL ADDRESS

In addition to providing your current contact information, you might also be asked to list your previous home address and phone number—especially if you've been living at your current residence for less than two years.

EDUCATIONAL BACKGROUND

Most applications require you to list high school and college information, including names, addresses, and telephone numbers of the institutions you attended. You also may be asked to indicate how many hours of course work you've completed at each educational level and what type of diploma, degree, or certificate was awarded to you. Dates of graduation and/or certification will be requested on most applications.

PREVIOUS WORK EXPERIENCES

Even if you have a resume available, many employers will still want you to list your previous work experiences on the official application. You'll need to have the starting and ending dates of your previous employment, the names and addresses of the companies or organizations you worked for, the names and phone numbers of your immediate supervisors, and a brief description of the work-related responsibilities associated with each job. You may also be asked to provide information about your salary history. Applications often require you to list both your starting and ending salary for each of your previous jobs.

PERSONAL AND PROFESSIONAL REFERENCES

Most applications request contact information (names, addresses, phone numbers and E-mail addresses) for both personal and professional references. Personal references are those people you would consider friends. The personal references you list on a job application should be people who know you quite well on an interpersonal level. Professional references can include former supervisors, teachers, or even coworkers who can attest to the quality of your work. Make sure you have handy all of the contact information for at least four or five personal and four or five professional references so that you can fully complete an application.

MISCELLANEOUS INFORMATION

Depending on the application, you might be asked to provide a variety of additional information, ranging from a list of your hobbies and interests to previous awards you've received and special talents and skills you possess.

THE EMPLOYMENT INTERVIEW

Probably the best job interview strategy that anyone could suggest is for you to attend a workshop on job-interviewing skills. Most college and university career centers offer interviewing skills workshops that can be especially effective for persons who lack interviewing experience. Some of these workshops even provide a videotaping service, in which a mock interview is taped so that you can see how you interact with someone during an interview situation. If you're unable to attend an interview skills workshop, then at the very least you should practice with a friend or family member. After running through a few "trials," you'll be much more prepared for an actual interview.

Another important point to consider is *always* to dress as professionally as possible when interviewing for a job—even for jobs that don't have strict dress codes. As mentioned before, the first impression you'll make with a prospective employer is going to last a long time. When hundreds of people are applying for a limited number of job openings, *everything* that you say and do plays an important role in whether or not you are offered the job.

It's also a good idea to go to an interview well prepared. Researching the company, for example, can give you a sense of what direction the company is moving in. This might help you anticipate the kinds of questions that you'll be asked during the interview. It also helps you come up with something interesting and meaningful to say when the interviewer asks you if *you* have any questions about the company or the position.

Make sure you'll be able to find the location of the interview prior to the actual day of your appointment. The last thing you want to do on your way to an interview is get lost. By finding out precisely where your interview is going to be held well in advance, you'll decrease some of the anxiety that's a natural part of interviewing.

Preparation is the key to successful job search strategies and application procedures. Even if several months or years will elapse before you'll be applying for a job, now is the time to prepare. If you haven't already started, begin learning *now* how you can go about finding job opportunities in the career you're pursuing. Put together a resume *today*—before you find yourself forced to develop one at the last minute. Collect all of the information you're likely to need to complete a job application and keep it organized in a file, updating it regularly. Attend job interview workshops whenever they're offered, and seek one-on-one assistance from a career counselor if you think it will help. The key is to be prepared for what lies ahead. Exactly how prepared you're going to be when the time comes to obtain a job is up to only one person . . . and that person is *you!*

Summary of Important Tips for Job Interview Preparation

- Attend job interview workshops.
- Practice interview skills with a family member or friend.
- Dress professionally (no matter what type of job it is).
- Find out about the company through research.
- Anticipate the questions you'll be asked and prepare answers accordingly.
- Be prepared to ask questions of the interviewer.
- Find out how to get to the interview location well in advance.

Appendix E

By completing a job satisfaction questionnaire, you'll be able to identify those aspects of your current job that are rewarding as well as those that contribute to dissatisfaction. The results will help you clarify the aspects of a job that most directly contribute to your career satisfaction. You can also use this exercise to predict how you *might* respond to *potential* occupations and the degree of satisfaction that a potential job is likely to provide.

PART I

GENERAL INFORMATION

Occupation: _____

How long have you worked for this company? _____

What previous positions have you held with the company?

_____

_____

What is your job title? _____

How long have you held your current position? _____

Briefly describe your work responsibilities (as you would on a resume):

_____

_____

_____

_____

_____

PART II

RATING YOUR CURRENT JOB SATISFACTION

1	2	3	4	5
not satisfied at all		*somewhat satisfied*		*extremely satisfied*

Using the scale shown above, rate your level of satisfaction with the following aspects of your job.

GENERAL WORKING CONDITIONS

_____ Hours worked each week

_____ Flexibility in scheduling

_____ Location of work

_____ Amount of paid vacation time/sick leave offered

PAY AND PROMOTION POTENTIAL

_____ Salary

_____ Opportunities for promotion

_____ Benefits (health insurance, life insurance, etc.)

_____ Job security

_____ Recognition for work accomplished

WORK RELATIONSHIPS

_____ Relationships with your coworkers

_____ Relationship(s) with your supervisor(s)

_____ Relationships with your subordinates (if applicable)

USE OF SKILLS AND ABILITIES

_____ Opportunity to utilize your skills and talents

_____ Opportunity to learn new skills

_____ Support for additional training and education

WORK ACTIVITIES

_____ Variety of job responsibilities

_____ Degree of independence associated with your work roles

_____ Adequate opportunity for periodic changes in duties

OTHER ASPECTS OF THE JOB RELATING TO YOUR LEVEL OF SATISFACTION

Review your ratings. List the items below for which your satisfaction level is a 4 or a 5:

_____

_____

_____

_____

_____

_____

These are the aspects of your current job with which you are generally satisfied. As you consider potential career changes in the future, make sure you take into account those things about your current job that are particularly satisfying.

Now list the items below for which your satisfaction level is a 1 or a 2.

_____

_____

_____

_____

_____

_____

These are the characteristics associated with your current job that are dissatisfying. They are the types of things that you'll want to avoid in any future career or occupational choice. You can gain a better understanding of what to look for in a future career by analyzing what it is that you dislike about your current job.

Bibliography

Ackley, K. M. (2000). *100 top internet job sites: Get wired, get hired in today's new job market.* Manassas Park, VA: Impact Publications.

Albert, K. A., & Luzzo, D. A. (1999). The role of perceived barriers in career development: A social cognitive perspective. *Journal of Counseling and Development, 77,* 431–436.

American Association for Retired Persons. (1994). *America's changing work force.* Washington, DC: Author.

Bandura, A. (1997). *Self-efficacy: The exercise of control.* New York: W. H. Freeman.

Brown, D. (1995). *Choosing your job upon retirement.* Lincolnwood, IL: VGM Books.

Brown, D. (1996). Brown's values-based, holistic model of career and life-role choices and satisfaction. In D. Brown, L. Brooks, & Associates (Eds.), *Career choice and development* (3rd ed.) (pp. 337–338). San Francisco: Jossey-Bass.

Brown, D., & Crace, R. K. (1995). Values in life role choices and outcomes: A conceptual model. *Career Development Quarterly, 44,* 211–223.

Cosgrove, H. (Ed.). (1996). *Encyclopedia of careers and vocational guidance* (10th ed.). Chicago: J. G. Ferguson.

Dictionary of occupational titles (4th ed.). (1991). Washington, DC: U.S. Department of Labor, Employment and Training Administration.

Farr, J. M. (1998). *The O*NET dictionary of occupational titles.* Indianapolis: JIST Works.

Field, S. (2000). *100 best careers for the 21st century* (2nd ed.). Stamford, CT: Arco Publications.

Hammer, A. L. (1993). *Introduction to type and careers.* Palo Alto, CA: Consulting Psychologists Press.

Harris-Bowlsbey, J., Dikel, M. R., & Sampson, Jr., J. P. (2002). *The internet: A tool for career planning* (2nd ed.). Columbus, OH: National Career Development Association.

Holland, J. L. (1997). *Making vocational choices* (3rd ed.). Upper Saddle River, NJ: Prentice-Hall.

Hoyt, K. B., & Lester, J. N. (1995). *Learning to work: The NCDA Gallup survey.* Alexandria, VA: National Career Development Association.

Kapes, J. T., Mastie, M. M., & Whitfield, E. A. (Eds.). (2001). *A counselor's guide to career assessment instruments* (4th ed.). Columbus, OH: National Career Development Association.

Krantz, L., & Lee, T. (2000). *Jobs rated almanac, 2001: The best and worst jobs.* New York: St. Martin's Press.

Luzzo, D. A. (1999). Identifying the career decision-making needs of nontraditional college students. *Journal of Counseling and Development,* 77, 135–140.

Maze, H., & Mayall, D. (2000). *Enhanced guide for occupational exploration: Descriptions for the 2,800 most important jobs.* Indianapolis: JIST Works.

Myers, I. B., & McCaulley, M. H. (1998). *Manual: A guide to the development and use of the Myers-Briggs Type Indicator* (3rd ed.). Palo Alto, CA: Consulting Psychologists Press.

National Board of Certified Counselors. (2001). *National directory of certified counselors.* Alexandria, VA: Author.

Occupational Information Network. (www.doleta.gov/programs/onet). Washington, DC: U. S. Department of Labor.

Occupational outlook handbook. (2002–2003). Washington, DC: U.S. Department of Labor.

Ostrow, S. (2001). *Joining the military.* Stamford, CT: Arco Publications.

Roe, A., & Lunneborg, P. W. (1990). Personality development and career choice. In D. Brown, L. Brooks, & Associates (Eds.), *Career choice and development: Applying contemporary theories to practice* (2nd ed., pp. 68–101). San Francisco: Jossey-Bass.

Super, D. E., Savickas, M. L., & Super, C. (1996). A life-span, life-space approach to career development. In D. Brown, L. Brooks, & Associates, *Career choice and development* (3rd ed.). San Francisco: Jossey-Bass.

Index